Faculty Service Roles and the Scholarship of Engagement

Kelly Ward

ASHE-ERIC Higher Education Report: Volume 29, Number 5
Adrianna J. Kezar, Series Editor

Prepared and published by

JOSSEY-BASS
A Wiley Imprint
www.josseybass.com

In cooperation with

ERIC Clearinghouse on Higher Education
The George Washington University
URL: www.eriche.org

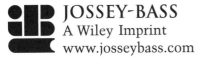

Association for the Study
of Higher Education
URL: www.tiger.coe.missouri.edu/~ashe

Graduate School of Education and Human Development
The George Washington University
URL: www.gwu.edu

Faculty Service Roles and the Scholarship of Engagement
Kelly Ward
ASHE-ERIC Higher Education Report: Volume 29, Number 5
Adrianna J. Kezar, Series Editor

This publication was prepared partially with funding from the Office of Educational Research and Improvement, U.S. Department of Education, under contract no. ED-99-00-0036. The opinions expressed in this report do not necessarily reflect the positions or policies of OERI or the Department.

ISSN 0884-0040   electronic ISSN 1536-0709   ISBN 0-7879-6350-X

The ASHE-ERIC Higher Education Report is part of the Jossey-Bass Higher and Adult Education Series and is published six times a year by Wiley Subscription Services, Inc., A Wiley Company, at Jossey-Bass, 989 Market Street, San Francisco, California 94103-1741.

For subscription information, see the Back Issue/Subscription Order Form in the back of this journal.

CALL FOR PROPOSALS: Prospective authors are strongly encouraged to contact Adrianna Kezar at (301) 405-0868 or kezar@wam.umd.edu.

Visit the Jossey-Bass Web site at **www.josseybass.com.**

Printed in the United States of America on acid-free recycled paper.

Executive Summary

Teaching, research, and service are commonly found in campus mission statements. But what this service means, for whom, and how it is rewarded remains unclear because service roles within higher education are not clearly defined and because people mean different things when they talk about faculty service. The need for clarity in this area is important given that contemporary calls for engagement and outreach as responses to challenges and movements in academia involve requests, demands, and increased attention to institutional and faculty service. Faculty are the foot soldiers of campus engagement with the community, so it is important for them to know what it means when the term *service* is used. Faculty are unlikely to engage in meaningful service if they are uncertain as to where it fits in larger schemas of work and how it is likely to be rewarded. In the light of calls for engagement, clear definitions of faculty service roles are necessary for productive discussion about the best way to create an engaged campus.

What Is the Origin of the Concept of Service?

Service has a variety of historical and contemporary components. Analysis of the historical development of higher education's service mission and faculty service roles provides a context for contemporary calls for campus involvement in service. A historical view is also a means to trace the genesis of the many definitions that surface when the word *service* is used in regard to institutional missions and faculty work.

The service mission of higher education is most strongly associated with the land grant movement of the nineteenth century. There is no doubt that this was an important turning point for the service role of higher education and connections between higher education, faculty expertise, and societal needs. However, the tradition of service has a long history in all sectors of higher education. Examination of the history of higher education through the lens of service shows how firmly embedded service is in the mission and actions of most colleges and universities. A historical review also shows the foundations of service in faculty work and how it has changed (and not changed) over time.

What Do We Mean When We Say "Faculty Service"?

Lack of understanding of the varied service roles of faculty can constrain faculty and institutional involvement in service. It is necessary to decipher what the different aspects of service mean, how they relate to faculty expertise, how they tie to campus missions, and how they are rewarded.

There are internal and external dimensions to service, and these two forms of service are distinct yet often lumped together under the rubric "faculty service." This creates a challenge because institutions themselves are not always clear about what it means for faculty to engage in service. *Internal service* refers to service to the institution as a means to conduct institutional business and service to the discipline as means to maintain disciplinary associations and their work. Internal service supports the internal functioning of the academic profession and higher education as a whole and is tied to the premise of shared governance. In contrast, *external service* is a means for institutions to communicate to multiple external audiences what it is that higher education does to meet societal needs. External service takes many forms, including extension, consulting, service-learning, and community and civic service. Common to all of these forms is faculty operating in contexts beyond the campus. Variability exists with regard to the extent that external service is tied to faculty disciplinary expertise and faculty enacting their community interests as individual citizens. The literature review makes clear that there is also variability in internal and external service roles depending on institutional type, discipline, rank, and demographics such as race and gender.

How Is Faculty Service Tied to Institutional Outreach?

Another aspect of definition is tied to what it means for a campus as a whole to enact its service mission. One way a campus does this is by reaching out to communities through making itself available as an intellectual resource for external audiences. Scholars concerned with the advancement of faculty service roles have tied faculty disciplinary expertise to this outreach and service mission. Service, then, is not an add-on to an already full faculty load but instead is a way for faculty to apply their disciplinary expertise to needs that exist beyond the campus. In this way, faculty can simultaneously meet their own needs for professional accomplishment and campus goals to be engaged with their communities. Goals for outreach cannot be met without faculty enacting their service roles.

What Is the Scholarship of Engagement?

Service is often seen as somehow outside the "real" work of scholars. This examination of the historical and contemporary roles of faculty service demonstrates instead that service is an important part of faculty life and must be understood and rewarded as such.

One way to make faculty service a more legitimate use of faculty resources is through a scholarship of engagement, where outreach and service activities are treated as scholarly activities in the same way that research always has been and teaching is increasingly. When faculty and administrators finally embrace a scholarship of engagement and acknowledge the important role of service in both the internal and external functioning and health of the campus, then faculty can begin to experience integrated academic lives, with teaching, research, and service reinforcing and supporting one another. The scholarship of engagement challenges faculty to view their work in addressing community needs as a means to connect and apply disciplinary expertise to needs that exist in the community and to integrate the lessons learned into their research and teaching.

How Can Campuses Move Toward a Scholarship of Engagement?

In spite of contemporary calls for the engaged campus, faculty members attempting to integrate engagement into their work can get caught between administrative and public calls for engagement and the realities of reward structures and staggering workloads. The literature review makes clear that efforts to connect campuses with community needs will remain unfulfilled without attention to the dilemmas like the workload one. Responses to dilemmas like these as well as recommendations for research and practice provide the basis for the conclusion of *Faculty Service Roles and the Scholarship of Engagement*.

Contents

Foreword

The academy continues to struggle to define the work of faculty. Recent pressures such as loss of faith by constituents, disjunctures between campus and community, cost concerns in higher education, dilemmas about curriculum, and student preparedness for the workforce have questioned traditional role definitions. But change is not easy; the forces affecting faculty roles are complex and nuanced. Also, faculty roles emerged historically to respond to societal issues and are deeply institutionalized.

Several ASHE-ERIC monographs over the past decade have examined the ways that faculty roles can be altered from a variety of perspectives, attempting to provide guidance to this multifaceted concept. Some authors have examined macro issues; an example is Sutton and Bergerson's monograph, *Faculty Compensation Systems* (2001). These authors explore the ways that rewards can influence faculty and institutional behavior. John Weidman, Darla Twale, and Elizabeth Leahy Stein (2001) reviewed the ways that the socialization of graduate and professional students affects the way they enact their role. At a more micro level, Barbara Walvoord and others, in *Academic Departments: How They Work, How They Change* (2000), examined the ways that departmental leadership can shape expectations around faculty work.

John Braxton, William Luckey, and Patricia Helland (2002) developed an ASHE-ERIC monograph that described the way that Boyer's *Scholarship Reconsidered* (1990) had altered the academy, specifically regarding faculty roles. Boyer placed more emphasis on the aspects of teaching and service and the ways these activities might be considered part of scholarship. This insightful

ASHE-ERIC monograph helps to examine both micro and macro forces that are affecting the institutionalization of Boyer's concept of "scholarship reconsidered" ten years after its introduction into the academy. Braxton and Associates find that Boyer's concept has been institutionalized to some degree. Although the scholarship of teaching is the area where institutions have made the fewest advances, many faculty, especially in applied or technical fields, are nevertheless developing scholarship that applies concepts and provides service to the field. There is much more work to be done to institutionalize new faculty roles and expanded conceptions of existing ones.

In this volume, Kelly Ward provides the needed guidance to continue the institutionalization of Boyer's concept and the general call for broadened views of faculty work. She also challenges traditional notions of service: the application of research to practice or service on campus committees and disciplinary societies. One of the major contributions of this monograph is that it defines and expands the definition of service to include the community and service-learning, newer notions of engagement. As Ward notes, "Engagement encompasses and expands upon the new conversations current in higher education that are trying to elevate and acknowledge faculty service roles and their connections to scholarship, faculty disciplinary expertise, and campus missions." The "new American scholar" integrates research and teaching and focuses on the ways these aspects are influenced by and influence the community outside the academy. This builds on and expands Boyer's work, especially around the notion of service.

This monograph provides a strong introduction to the service role of faculty and the concept of engagement through a detailed historical review of the faculty role. Internal and external service roles are described, with a focus on the ways that these are communicated and rewarded within different campus contexts. The attention to institutional differences is important in a diverse system of higher education that has unique cultures and structures. The monograph ends by providing examples of campuses that serve as exemplars in linking service to scholarship and incorporating it into promotion and tenure guidelines. Ward asks the tough questions: Given the prevalence of traditional research in many reward structures, isn't encouraging faculty to be more fully involved in "new" forms of scholarships irresponsible? Doesn't the call for the scholarship of engagement just mean more work for a faculty that is increasingly time deprived? Is it fair to ask faculty to do one more thing?

This monograph is important reading for all constituents in higher education: policymakers, administrators, and individual faculty alike.

Adrianna J. Kezar
Series Editor

Acknowledgments

This monograph would not have been possible without the assistance of my graduate assistants at Oklahoma State University, Amy Caswell, Ramona Fox, and Kitty Hankins, the editorial assistance of Gene Solomon, the comments of the anonymous reviewers, and the skillful combination of patience and prodding by Adrianna Kezar. I hereby express my thanks to all of you.

Contemporary Contexts for Service: The Engaged Campus

MANY SOCIAL AND ACADEMIC forces have led to questions and concerns about the role of higher education in American life. Publication of *A Nation at Risk* (1983) heightened the public's concern about whether higher education was doing its job to educate the citizenry by pointing to rates of illiteracy, job force ill preparedness, and higher education lacking in K–12 teacher preparation. The national service movement of the 1990s that created AmeriCorps and the Corporation for National Service also have had consequences for higher education, mostly by way of resources to improve higher education's relationship with society through learn-and-serve programs and the capacity to develop greater connections between town and gown. In addition to these external forces, internal forces within higher education have pressured it to reconsider its position. Concerns about curriculum and faculty work in addition to changes in public support of higher education have led the faculty and administrators who are central to the functioning of higher education to question the insular and autonomous nature of higher education.

In response to these calls for greater involvement in the common wealth, some have proposed a new vision for colleges and universities: an engaged campus that is committed to its students and faculty and fulfilling its traditional role in teaching and training students and citizens, but also newly committed to serving the communities and constituencies that surround and support it. This notion of engagement refers to redesigned and reenvisioned teaching, research, extension, and service functions that are sympathetically and productively involved with the communities that campuses serve, however

---

those communities are defined (Kellogg Commission, 1999b; Ramaley, 2000a; Saltmarsh and Hollander, 1999; Votruba, 1996). Engagement is a highly positive step toward reestablishing what higher education is intended to be: a community of scholars, serving both internal and external audiences in addition to the academic and the public good (Boyer, 1994; Kellogg Commission, 1999b, 2000).

Because a major aspect of the engaged campus is serving and working with a variety of communities, administrators and faculty have begun to think and talk about strengthening and renewing the service aspect of university and faculty life. These discussions can be challenging, in part because service can have many definitions in an academic context: service to a discipline, a department, a college, a committee, a student, or any one of a variety of communities in addition to having audiences internal and external to higher education. Some of this confusion arises because the service missions of colleges and universities have grown and changed throughout the history of American higher education.

A majority of college and university campuses reference service in their mission statements, and typically their faculty promotion and tenure guidelines speak of service as well (Crosson, 1983; Lynton, 1995). Many activities are classified as service, ranging from departmental committee work to private consulting to lending expertise for community causes. This nebulous description of service can minimize the importance of the service role of faculty work. Service to the institution gets confused with service to community, which in turn gets confused with service to the larger society (Fear and Sandmann, 1995). Because service is vaguely understood and defined, it is often viewed as less meaningful and important than the more easily defined (and rewarded) roles of teaching and research. In addition, the many aspects of academic service raise questions for administrators and faculty. Should faculty be engaged in and rewarded for community service? How are internal and external service evaluated? What constitutes

Because service is vaguely understood and defined, it is often viewed as less meaningful and important than the more easily defined (and rewarded) roles of teaching and research.

public service? How does the service mission of the university translate to faculty roles? Is an activity service if it is compensated or if it is for a private entity?

These and other questions have attracted the attention of faculty and administrators looking to enliven their service missions in response to public calls for accountability and productivity. These leaders see service as a means to respond to criticism from the public and policymakers in ways that are congruent with the service role and mission of higher education. What is unclear and in need of definition, however, is precisely what the service role of a college campus is and what it might become, as well as how faculty might best use and perform service to further the education of their students and the missions of their institutions.

Motivated by larger calls for colleges and universities to be engaged with their communities, this monograph seeks to address some of the questions that remain unanswered with regard to the service role of faculty and the institutions where they work and to provide a comprehensive overview of the service categories associated with faculty work and how they are linked to engagement. This overview helps to clarify what service is, how it evolved historically, where it fits in faculty work, how it can be evaluated, and how it ties to the engaged campus. Furthermore, the monograph offers clear links between service and scholarship as a means to embed service in the scholarly roles of faculty. Such a linkage has the potential to make service a part of the scholarly role and not an add-on to the already consuming workload of faculty (Finkelstein, Seal, and Schuster, 1998).

The monograph is timely; many campuses are grappling with attempts to expand their service roles effectively while involving faculty fully in this effort. Coherent expansion of service requires that it be clearly defined and that expectations and rewards for faculty are clearly expressed. The success of creating a service culture for faculty is tied to institutional support and the ability of institutions to define and reward service (Burack, 2000; Singleton, Burack, and Hirsch, 1997; Ramaley, 2000a). Furthermore, distinctions and definitions of service internal and external to campus must be clear, so that faculty can determine what is required of them and how service is tied to the work of a scholar.

The Many Meanings of Service

No research on service (or engagement or outreach) can progress far without a word or two on the topic of definition. Given the current emphasis on service and the many meanings this term can have on a college campus, it is important to add clarity to the conversation. Lack of understanding of the service role of faculty (and its many meanings) can constrain faculty and institutional involvement (Holland, 1997, 1999; Ramaley, 2000a). In this monograph, I use the term *service* to refer to the *activities* that comprise the service role (for example, serving on campus committees, serving the discipline, service to the community, service-learning). The monograph is dedicated to deciphering what these different aspects of service mean, how they relate to faculty expertise, how they tie to campus missions, and how they are rewarded. Furthermore, the monograph examines both internal and external service roles to help clarify the differences between these two forms of service, each different from the other yet often lumped together under the rubric "faculty service." *Service,* then, is the word that is used to define the activities that comprise this aspect of faculty work, that is, what faculty actually do when they engage in service.

I use the term *engagement* to encompass and expand on the new conversations current in higher education that seek to elevate and acknowledge faculty service roles and their connections to scholarship, faculty disciplinary expertise, and campus missions. Engagement is an organizing concept that encompasses faculty service roles and recognizes the possibility that these roles have a place in faculty scholarship (Sandmann and others, 2000). Engagement, in particular, is used throughout the literature as a concept more than a particular activity. Engagement is used in two ways: (1) to define a relationship with the community that is grounded in mutuality and respect, while acknowledging the complexities that exist in campus and community relationships (Hollander and Saltmarsh, 2000; Ramaley, 2000a), and (2) to define the connection between faculty service activities and disciplinary expertise, that is, how a faculty member's expertise affects his or her service activities and how these service activities can influence disciplinary expertise and scholarship (Boyer, 1996; Ramaley, 2000a). The scholarship of engagement challenges faculty to view their work in addressing community needs as a means to connect and apply disciplinary expertise to needs that exist in the community and integrate the lessons learned into their research and teaching (Sandmann and others, 2000).

Scholars (Boyer, 1990; Fear and Sandmann, 1995; Lynton, 1995) concerned with the advancement of faculty service roles have focused on definitions of service, outreach, and engagement. Although no universals exist to guide the nomenclature of how professional service is distinct from outreach or engagement, there are some guiding principles that will be highlighted throughout this monograph. The ultimate goal of this work is to clarify the definitions and terminology associated with the movement toward academic service as an activity that supports engagement, in an effort to lend credence to these aspects of faculty work and institutional mission.

Forces Shaping Contemporary Calls for Engagement

Calls for institutional engagement have been shaped by internal and external forces that call on colleges and universities to rethink their roles and their relationships with communities beyond the campus. These forces include social and academic challenges and trends.

Social and Academic Challenges

Higher education faces challenges on many fronts. Some of these challenges have always dogged the academy; some are new. Current calls for engagement have been framed in terms of creating systems of higher education that respond to the many challenges that face higher education. Based on a reading of scholarly and popular commentary about higher education, the message is clear: the public has lost faith in higher education, and higher education is part of the problem instead of the solution (Astin, 1994; Boyer, 1996; Harkavy and Puckett, 1994; Hirsch and Weber, 1999; Spanier, 2001).

American higher education has operated with a great deal of internal and external autonomy throughout much of its history (Altbach, 1995; Lynton and Elman, 1987). For the most part, the academy has been left alone to perform the job of educating students and citizens. The Morrill Act (1862) and the land grant universities were generally supported for the services and students they provided to the nation. Government programs to support higher education like the GI Bill (1944) and the National Defense Education Act (1958), which supported students in the *Sputnik* era, were enormously popular. Higher education instilled hope and confidence in the populace. Today, the general support and faith in higher education no longer exists (Koldony, 1998).

Following are some of the challenges facing higher education. Collectively these concerns contribute to a public distrust of higher education.

Disjunctures Between Campus and Community. Many people outside the academy see higher education as "aloof and out of touch, arrogant and out of date" (Kellogg Commission, 1999b, p. 20). Colleges and universities are often viewed as disconnected from the urgent concerns of the day and the concerns of the communities that surround and support campuses (Harkavy, 1999). These accusations may or may not be accurate, but much of this critical perception of higher education arises because the academy has tended to be internally focused and has failed to communicate well what it does for its community and society as a whole (Altbach, 1995; Harkavy, 1993, 1999; Udell, 1990). Furthermore, higher education has been accused of not being a good neighbor by living in a community yet not contributing to its well-being (Harkavy, 1993, 1999; Harkavy and Puckett, 1994).

Cost Concerns About Higher Education. Faith in higher education has eroded as the cost of higher education has risen (Altbach, 1995; Kolodny, 1998). The rising cost draws increased scrutiny and criticism from those who fund the system and pay the bills: legislators and students and their parents. The public sees high price tags on education but often has no clear understanding of what it is that higher education does with the money (Kellogg Commission, 1999b). Furthermore, public university systems, under increased scrutiny, have been and are accused of wasteful spending (Altbach, 1995; Kolodny, 1998). The net result is diminished public support and public funding, which has led to massive increases in tuition costs, further eroding public support for public and private higher education. Public funding for higher education continues to diminish to the point where many "public" institutions of higher education receive less than 50 percent of their budgets from public coffers (Kellogg Commission, 1999b). In essence, many people now view a college education, long held as a public good, as a private benefit that parents, and not the public, should pay for (Altbach, 1995; Boyer, 1996). Cost concerns affect private and public education as tuition soars.

Calls for Accountability. Higher education as an organization has enjoyed an autonomy that is now under question. In short, "the call for accountability is heating up" (Spanier, 2001, p. 4). Fiscal stress has led to greater scrutiny of higher education spending (Altbach, 1995). As public dollars diminish and higher education sees increases in spending and asks for more money, administrators need to be clear about campus spending. On many campuses today, greater record-keeping measures are common, as administrators attempt to track and justify expenditures. Administrators, legislators, and concerned citizens have called for more accountability by demanding direct benefits from educational expenditures, such as a skilled workforce and applied research. They want to see public benefits of allocated money. The net result is concern about what it is that higher education does and for whom (Astin, 1994; Cohen, 1998). This concern emanates not only from external audiences but from internal ones as well. Academic administrators want to know how their faculty are communicating teaching effectiveness and research quality, among other issues, to the public (Altbach, 1995; Tierney, 1998).

Concerns About Campus Morals and Politics. News programs, newspapers, and magazines often feature stories about questionable academic spending, the moral turpitude of professors, and excessive drinking among students (Kennedy, 1997; Kolodny, 1998). Other stories highlight rallies or riots focused on sexuality, religion, race, or athletic programs. In addition, discussions of curriculum often leave parents suspicious that their children are being exposed to radical, liberal, and ideological ideas by radical and liberal faculty members (Kolodny, 1998; Tierney and Bensimon, 1996). "Higher education has been castigated for not devoting its energies to moral education" (Cohen, 1998, p. 414). Some view higher education as an amoral enterprise.

Questions About Curriculum and Student Preparedness for the Workforce. Concerns about what it is that students learn and by whom they are taught tie to worries about the cost of higher education, and leave the public (and particularly parents) anxious that students are being poorly prepared for future employability, while paying a high price for the privilege. Kolodny (1998) explains:

> *Public discussions of higher education at the end of the 1990s have come to be dominated by two propositions. The first proposition asserts that the rising costs of college and university tuition must point to inflated faculty salaries and to wastefulness and poor management on the part of higher education administrators. The second proposition asserts that traditional core subjects, especially in the humanities, have been displaced by radical new curricula that undermine students' regard for Western civilization and that call into question all standards and values* [p. 47].

Increasingly, the focus on higher education is on what it produces, specifically students who are employable in a market economy.

The second proposition taken a step further points to concerns about what it is that students are learning (or not) in higher education and if what they are learning will get them a job. Increasingly, the focus on higher education is on what it produces, specifically students who are employable in a market economy (Aronowitz, 2001). Criticisms are leveled when higher education is perceived as failing its mission by producing graduates with esoteric knowledge but lacking specific skill sets to find jobs (Cohen, 1998; Kolb, 1984).

Concerns and Questions About Faculty Work. Faculty are often characterized as leading "privileged, protected lives, often pursuing agendas incongruent with students' needs—in a word, say their critics, out of touch with the 'real world'" (Finkelstein and others, 1998, p. 2). Faculty recognize the many roles that make up their positions: days filled with preparing for and teaching classes, meeting with students, advising, grant writing and research, writing for publication, involvement in governance on campus, and participation in meetings both on and off campus, to name a few of the activities that fill the faculty work week. Contrary to public belief, faculty work long hours and are notoriously underpaid as highly educated professionals (Tierney and Bensimon, 1996). Outsiders, however, tend to view faculty as highly paid eccentrics, protected by tenure, who engage in esoteric and self-centered research, assign teaching to assistants, and infuse the curriculum with their political agendas (Kolodny, 1998; Sykes, 1988; Tierney and Bensimon, 1996). These concerns about faculty work emanate from a general misunderstanding of what faculty members do and from higher education's inability to communicate effectively about faculty work (Chaffee, 1998; Hirsch and Weber, 1999).

Social and Academic Trends

Higher education is being challenged to respond to problems that exist in the larger social milieu. In addition to these challenges, trends in higher education have shifted, affecting the landscape of colleges and universities. These movements have focused increased concern on campus and community relationships and campus involvement in issues beyond the campus. Some of these trends predate the challenges already set out; others have been affected by the challenges facing higher education. In each case, however, the impact has been to contribute to the movement toward greater community involvement for higher education.

Paradigm Shifts in Teaching and Learning. Although college students are no strangers to mundane lectures, there have been shifts in classroom contexts that give way to approaches to teaching and learning that are more experiential and collaborative. These classrooms shift the onus for learning from the instructor as the sole source of knowledge to students as partners in the learning process and experiences beyond the classroom for what they can add to student learning (Kolb, 1984; McKeachie, 2002). These shifting teaching and learning paradigms mean more opportunities for students to engage in research opportunities, internships, and service-learning (Spanier, 2001).

National Service. The 1990 National and Community Service Act and the founding of the Corporation for National Service in 1993 have had a profound impact on higher education's response to community needs. The act and the corporation have challenged higher education to rethink its civic roles and have been instrumental in providing support to higher education to bolster this involvement, primarily through expanded opportunity for service-learning (Harkavy, 1993). The AmeriCorps program has been instrumental in supporting community service. It provides remuneration to those involved in community service with educational awards to support higher education, and it places AmeriCorps members on campus to develop campus involvement with communities and in communities to support their involvement in higher education. Collectively, these initiatives have put higher education in closer contact with its communities and brought higher education's attention to community service on campus. The use of federal work-study funds to place students in the community has also put higher education in closer contact with its communities.

Association Involvement in Engagement Initiatives. We do not have to look far to see a spate of involvement by academic associations in outreach initiatives (Bringle, Games, and Malloy, 1999). Associations of colleges and universities (such as the Council of Independent Colleges and American Council of Education) have been involved in leading the institutions they represent in the conversation on engagement. In addition, disciplinary associations (among them, the Modern Language Association and the American Chemical Society) have taken on issues associated with service and community involvement as a means to guide faculty in their service activities (Zlotkowski, 2000, 2001). Perhaps most important has been Campus Compact, an institutional membership organization of over eight hundred campuses dedicated to reinvigorating the service role of higher education. Founded in 1985, Campus Compact has become a prominent voice in increasing the civic capacity of higher education through student, faculty, and administrative involvement in community concerns.

(Dis)connections Between Common and Higher Education. Recent attention has focused on the relationship between higher education and K–12 education, particularly in the area of teacher preparation. The No Child Left Behind Act of 2001 calls on higher education to take a more active role in remediating problems that exist in schools through the work of postsecondary schools of education. In addition, the 1999 report of the American Council on Higher Education, *To Touch the Future: Transforming the Way Teachers Are Taught,* calls on colleges and university presidents to take action in the area of teacher education. The trend toward more synergy between higher education and K–12 education suggests the need for higher education to be more responsive to larger educational needs and the needs of youth for quality education (Brown, 1994). Higher education is being asked to examine its role in teacher preparation and educational reform more closely (Zemsky, 1994).

Increasing Use of Part-Time Faculty. The number of part-time faculty is on the rise. This trend affects the functioning of higher education in two ways that are germane to the topic of service. First, these faculty are typically less involved in campus and disciplinary service than their full-time colleagues. The result is that full-time faculty find their service responsibilities correspondingly greater or that administrators do the service work of faculty, thus diminishing faculty involvement in shared governance. Second, nontenure-track faculty (many of whom are part time) are more likely to be involved in service-learning and to be more involved in their community (Antonio, Astin, and Cress, 2000).

Engagement as a Response to These Challenges and Trends

The concept of engagement evolves from the work of Boyer (1990) and Rice (1996b) and their call for new definitions of scholarship to shape the work of the "new American scholar." Higher education's response to an expanded view of scholarship suggests that the contemporary context for higher education is ripe for change. A myopic focus on research in faculty work has created skewed and outmoded reward structures and campuses that are self-centered (Boyer, 1990, 1996; Fairweather, 1996; Harkavy, 1999; Rice, 1996b; Tierney, 1998; Tierney and Bensimon, 1996).

Higher education's response to an expanded view of scholarship suggests that the contemporary context for higher education is ripe for change.

Scholarship Reconsidered (Boyer, 1990) offers a model for expanding traditional definitions of scholarship that more aptly define what it is that faculty do. Boyer's model for scholarship has created unprecedented interest in redefining faculty roles and rewards and institutional missions (Braxton, Luckey, and Helland, 2002). These scholarships (and corresponding categories from traditional faculty work) are as follows: discovery (research), integration (synthesis), teaching (teaching), and application (service). The scholarship of application, in particular, has captured the attention of those looking to validate faculty service roles and the important role they play in engaging academe with the issues and concerns of larger society. Although Boyer's work offers categories that divide "intellectual functions," Boyer's legacy is in acknowledging that all the forms of scholarship "dynamically interact, forming an independent whole" (Boyer, 1990, p. 25).

An additional category of scholarship—the scholarship of engagement—also stems from Boyer's work. Engagement grows out of the notion of the scholarship of application. It supersedes the scholarship of application as well, in that the scholarship of engagement provides a model to integrate all the other aspects of scholarship. That is, it is possible through an integrated view of faculty work to see that all work can be categorized as the scholarship of engagement (Sandmann and others, 2000).

In addition to the scholarship of engagement as an organizing framework for faculty work, campuses as a whole have looked to engagement as a way to define and characterize institutional missions and respond to the challenges facing higher education today (Bringle, Games, and Malloy, 1999). The academic landscape—campuses and wider disciplinary circles—is filled with calls for engagement and the wish for higher education to be more in touch with societal needs and more responsive to societal problems (Kellogg Commission, 1999a, 1999b, 2000; Hollander, 1998; Hollander and Saltmarsh, 2000; Spanier, 2001). No one has to look far to see conference themes, special issues of journals, meetings of administrators, and special summits on service and what this all means to be an engaged campus. The term *engagement* is used as a response to a general uneasiness many in higher education are feeling about the nexus of higher education's past, present, and future and how this composite history plays a role in society.

In a campus focused on engagement, boundaries between campus and community, knowledge and dissemination, town and gown, research and application are blurred. Engaged campuses are those "institutions that have redesigned their teaching, research, and extension and service functions to become more sympathetically and productively involved with their communities, however community may be defined" (Kellogg Commission, 1999b, p. 10).

Presidents, provosts, regents, and faculty have begun to recognize engagement with communities as a means to connect the university and the college with the communities with which they are involved. This process of partnering and cooperating in the solution of problems and the delivery of education has stretched the boundaries of traditional notions of the academy. As the college and university community has reached out to the community at large, it has also recognized that partnerships work in two directions (Maurrasse, 2001; Magrath, 1999; Ramaley, 2000a; Sandmann and others, 2000). These partnerships, born of the need to connect with the community, have also given the community a chance to connect with, challenge, and change the university.

The lines drawn between "us" and "them" are less clearly defined in a framework of engagement. The engaged campus is one where the campus as a whole takes seriously its role as a citizen to its community and one where reciprocal relationships and partnerships with communities are honored (Ayers and Ray, 1996; Kellogg Commission, 1999b; Maurrasse, 2001; Ward and Wolf-Wendel, 2000). Typically, society sees one role of higher education as to educate a citizenry, and there is an implied citizenship and participation of higher education in those expectations. Until recently, however, higher education has not been very introspective about what it means to be a citizen, a contributing member of society, and a good neighbor (Harkavy, 1999). Higher education does meet vital public needs through its teaching and research missions. However, it is how these missions have been enacted that has been the cause of criticism. For a long time, higher education believed that its service

> In a campus focused on engagement, boundaries between campus and community, knowledge and dissemination, town and gown, research and application are blurred.

mission was fulfilled simply in its presence—by providing economic, knowledge, and educational benefits to its community (Boyer, 1990). This inherited concept implies a one-way process where the institution gives expertise to the community by virtue of its existence (Kellogg Commission, 1999b; Sandmann and others, 2000). This is clearly no longer the case in an era of calls for greater accountability and criticisms of higher education for being self-centered and disconnected from reality—a place where students become credentialed as a step to individual pursuits and where faculty live isolated esoteric lives protected by tenure (Altbach, 1995; Boyer, 1994, 1996; Kolodny, 1998; Finkelstein and others, 1998).

Additional social factors encourage engagement as well. Some argue that with diminished roles of government in communities, it is higher education institutions that will pick up some of the societal needs previously met by government programs, as colleges and universities offer sorely needed resources, including an educated workforce, research, faculty expertise, and libraries (Checkoway, 1997, 2000; Ramaley, 2000a, 2000b; Taylor, 1997). It is in this way that higher education has looked to engagement as a way to respond to the many criticisms leveled against it.

The engaged campus is characterized by administrative and presidential commitment to community involvement, faculty research and teaching tied to community aims, student involvement in community service and the public domain, and, for campuses as a whole, building collaborative relationships based on reciprocity and mutual respect (Ayers and Ray, 1996; Hollander, 1998; Maurrasse, 2001; Magrath, 1999). The engaged campus builds on higher education's contribution to society and to a history of higher education that has always been "inextricably intertwined" with the larger purposes of American society (Boyer, 1994; Ehrlich, 1995; Magrath, 1999). Furthermore, the engaged campus reorients the core functions of academe—teaching, research, and service—to focus on the needs of local communities (Saltmarsh and Hollander, 1999). Engagement calls on colleges and universities to be good citizens (Bringle, Games, and Malloy, 1999).

The engaged campus must strive to accomplish the following three goals:

1. *It must be organized to respond to the needs of today's students and tomorrow's, not yesterday's.*

2. *It must enrich students' experiences by bringing research and engagement into the curriculum and offering practical opportunities for students to prepare for the world they will enter.*

3. *It must put its critical resources (knowledge and expertise) to work on the problems the communities it serves face (Kellogg Commission, 1999b, p. 10).*

In short, the engaged campus goes beyond a one-way relationship of knowledge flowing outward from the university to a relationship that acknowledges synergy between knowledge in and knowledge out and one where the community voice is part of the process (Spanier, 2001). The engaged campus and the engaged faculty member put knowledge to work (Spanier, 2001; Magrath, 1999).

The Role of Service in Engagement

The three facets of a faculty member's job in the modern university are teaching, research, and service. When people talk about teaching, they tend to be in agreement on what they mean. Faculty are first and foremost teachers; teaching is part of the very definition of what it means to be a faculty member. As modern roles for faculty have evolved, another part of the faculty role that is clear, at least to those on the inside of academe, is research: faculty are creators of knowledge and information (Altbach, 1995; Boyer, 1990). When people refer to the service role of faculty, however, what this involves is less clear (Berberet, 1999; O'Meara, 1997). This uncertainty may be entirely appropriate, as the service role of faculty is expansive and often vaguely defined (Boice, 2000; Fear and Sandmann, 1995).

Unlike the teaching and research aspects of the faculty role and university work, service that is focused on outreach and application can help establish direct links between the work of the university and the needs of the public (Lynton, 1995). Service, depending on the time and place, can mean service to the profession, service to the community, service to the institution, service to the public sector, service to the private sector, or service to society in general. Some of these service areas are tied to academic specialization and can easily be defined as "scholarly"; some are not categorized so easily. The problem for many institutions is how to acknowledge and reward service, an issue that needs to be addressed if campuses want to fully use faculty service as a means to realize institutional goals for engagement. It is important to look at both internal and external service in this context, as calls for engagement recognize the service role of faculty in all its complexity. In short, the engaged campus is supported in part by faculty internal and external service roles.

This monograph seeks to add clarity to faculty service roles by describing what it is that faculty do to meet institutional and disciplinary needs (that is, internal service) and the service that faculty do that extends their expertise beyond the campus (that is, external service). It links service to scholarship using the rubric of the scholarship of engagement. Just as the scholarship of teaching elevates the work that faculty do as teachers to the scholarly realm by tying it to disciplinary expertise, the scholarship of engagement has the potential to heighten awareness of faculty service roles by tying service to expertise in the discipline and the needs that exist both internal and external to the campus. In making the case for more awareness to the scholarship of engagement, I recognize that this can lead to many dilemmas for campuses and individual faculty. This monograph responds to these challenges by looking to the lessons learned by research on faculty service and looking to campus examples and providing direction for the future. Given the long tradition of service and outreach in American higher education, we start with an overview of the service role of campuses and faculty.

The Legacy of Service
in Higher Education

WHAT IS THE PURPOSE of higher education? What goals should colleges and universities attempt to pursue? What obligations do colleges and universities have to society? What role do faculty play in translating these roles? Responses to these questions can be found, in part, by examining the historical evolution of faculty roles.

To understand contemporary calls for engagement and a scholarship of service more fully requires a grasp of the historical efforts of higher education to serve multiple publics and the faculty's role in providing that service. Although the service mission of higher education is most strongly associated with the public college and land grant movements of the mid-nineteenth century, the tradition of service has a long history in all sectors of higher education. A firm understanding of these traditions is needed to ground today's calls for engagement and an enlivened faculty role. "We need to turn, however briefly, to the unique past of American higher education if we wish to deepen our understanding of the unique present and likely future of its core profession" (Clark, 1987, p. xxiii).

The tradition of service has a long history in all sectors of higher education.

This chapter approaches the history of service by examining the institutional mission of higher education as it relates to service and the emergence of faculty service roles. This is done by separating higher education and its tradition of service into five general eras: the colonial college, the denominational college, the research university, mass education, and the contemporary era.

The schema for these eras is informed by the work of Cohen (1998), Brubacher and Rudy (1997), and Geiger (1999).

The Colonial College (1636–1770)

The colonial period began with the founding of Harvard College in 1636 and continued until the political and social landscape changed and started to diversify around the time of the American Revolution.

Institutional Mission

Higher education in colonial America was modeled after European (mostly, though not exclusively, English) forms, but quickly became a unique system (Cremin, 1970). Harvard College was founded in 1636 in Cambridge, Massachusetts, to "advance piety, civility, and learning" (Cremin, 1970, p. 48), primarily through the classical training of clergy and civil servants, and it became the model for other colonial colleges (Brubacher and Rudy, 1997). In 1693, William and Mary was chartered to prepare clergy for the Anglican church, "civilize" Indians, and prepare public and civil servants (Cohen, 1998). From its inception, higher education in the American colonies had as its focus socialization of the young for positions of leadership in the church, education in the classics and Christian doctrine, and, ultimately, preparation of students as public servants (Cohen, 1998). Given the close ties between church and state in the colonies, students were often prepared to assume positions in both spheres (Cremin, 1970).

Even the mission to civilize Indian students at Harvard, William and Mary, and Dartmouth had a service orientation to it. Although more recent research reveals that the enterprise was ignoble, deceptive, and questionable with its intent to Christianize Indians and to "civilize and remake them in the image of the European" (Wright, 1988, p. 73) against their wishes, it was undertaken in the name of service. Wright (1988) has examined the stated pious goals of educating Indian youth and found that these aims were dishonorable and focused more on the queen's desires than those of the natives. Even today, some of what is done in the name of service can be exploitative and more focused on advancing the agenda of higher education and not those it intends to serve—part of the legacy of service requiring vigilance (Calderon, 1999; Kahne and Westheimer, 1996; Marullo and Edwards, 2000; Maurrasse, 2001; Oakes and Rogers, 2001).

The early colonial college, with strict adherence to Christian doctrine and the classical curriculum, evolved to include a more rationalist view of knowledge and began to focus on the study of political philosophy, mathematics, physics, chemistry, and geology (Cohen, 1998). There were also changes in how students took their classes. Initially, curriculum was prescribed, with all students exposed to uniform study and faculty with general knowledge. Courses of study began to change as faculty specialized (the beginning of academic specialization) and students could focus on particular interest (the beginning of student majors) (Cohen, 1998; Cremin, 1970).

The colonial college era also saw proponents who countered the prevailing religious focus of the times. Benjamin Franklin as early as 1750 wanted to see higher education be a "more useful culture of young minds" and to see curriculum develop a more rational approach by including training in agriculture and commerce (Kerr, 1963). Thomas Jefferson was also a strong proponent of a more broadened view of higher education in terms of both offerings and access (Brubacher and Rudy, 1997). These ideas, however, did not set firmly until the next century.

Faculty Roles

In the early colonial college, the teaching profession was "struggling to be born" (Cohen, 1998, p. 25), with tutors hired for their religious commitment rather than their scholarly or teaching abilities (Boyer, 1990; Finkelstein, 1984). Faculty were tutors, typically recent graduates, who were awaiting positions as clergy, and so their tenures tended to be short. The assumption was clear: those who had recently graduated could teach all subjects leading to the degree (Finkelstein, 1984). Faculties were small in number and usually consisted of the president (who also taught) and two or three tutors (Cohen, 1998). The colonial college environment was rather intimate, with tutors not only teaching classes and leading recitations but also spending entire days with students, even sharing living quarters (Cohen, 1998; Finkelstein, 1984).

College teaching as a profession took time to evolve. In the last half of the eighteenth century, a core of faculty replaced some of the tutors, thus establishing a professoriat (Finkelstein, 1984). Finkelstein (1984) describes the development of professorships as the result of "philanthropic bequest." The first, in 1721, was a professor of divinity at Harvard and the second, in 1727, was in mathematics and natural philosophy (Geiger, 1999). The creation of professorships established specialization, and the very first seeds of the academic disciplines were planted. Upon the hiring of specialized professors, the faculty then was made up of young tutors who taught all subjects to a single class (typically for all four years), with mainly older professors who taught in their specialty areas. Tutors, because they were recent graduates, were usually hired from inside, and professors with some postbaccalaureate training were hired from outside the institution (Cohen, 1998). The service element of these early faculty positions of tutors and professors was tied to their efforts to educate students while being paid low wages. In some instances, early faculty were like "volunteers engaged in public service" (Cohen, 1998, p. 27). These early teachers were dedicated to shaping and acculturating the youth of a young country for the love of the profession and not for the salary they were paid.

The Denominational College (1770–1860)

Denominational colleges were those affiliated with religious denominations. They are the forerunners to today's church-affiliated liberal arts colleges.

Institutional Mission

The denominational college appeared as the young nation expanded rapidly west. As new territories were acquired and towns settled, higher education had a prominent place on the landscape. The denominational college was founded on many principles tied to service.

Higher education offered developing communities an educated citizenry and the economic benefits of a college located in a community. Colleges attracted students and faculty, who contributed to the economy of a particular locale (Potts, 1977). Students were drawn from local communities, and those communities in turn supported higher education. Colleges and their communities were closely aligned. Furthermore, unlike the colonial colleges that largely provided education for the elite, denominational colleges were likely to enroll a more diverse cross-section of society, with students from the middle- and lower middle-class ranges of society (Potts, 1977). Geographical proximity was key to this diversity in enrollments. Students who had previously been denied enrollment to the colonial colleges based on location now had higher education more readily accessible, both financially and geographically (Potts, 1977).

As communities proliferated, so did religious denominations and affiliate campuses, putting higher education in closer contact with its communities. Most of these colleges were established in small communities to serve populations in the new West. Most relevant to the service mission of higher education during this era are the new alliances forged between campus and community. In order to bring campuses to particular locations, educators and communities had to act together to establish campuses (Potts, 1977). The geographical expansion of colleges also expanded curricular offerings in order to be more responsive to community needs and meet the need for more studies in scientific areas. As the nineteenth century wore on, most denominational colleges maintained the classical core curriculum and added studies in English and science, in addition to classes considered more practical, in areas such as business and teaching (Geiger, 1999). Curriculum expansion offered a way for higher education to respond to community needs.

As communities formed in the West, a sign of development and progress was the presence of a college. College and community interactions were vital to the success of the denominational college in the early nineteenth century (Brubacher and Rudy, 1997). These colleges were not ivory towers; rather, they were sites of economic and cultural gain and intimately involved with the community (Potts, 1977). Many who never attended college but who nonetheless saw the social benefits of higher education supported these institutions. This created the ideal of higher education as a public good and exposed higher education to many people for whom higher education had been elusive. As Potts (1977) points out, "Seeing the denominational college as a link to community provides us with a clearer understanding of the degree to which early nineteenth-century colleges were locally prominent, economically accessible, academically attractive, and generally popular in the eyes of a significant and increasing portion of the American public" (p. 157).

The presence of a college also had significant economic benefits, resulting at times in bidding wars over campuses. Communities tried to make themselves attractive and accessible to higher education interests (Potts, 1977).

Although not a denominational college, Rensselaer Polytechnic Institute, founded in 1834 in Troy, New York, had a profound impact on the direction of higher education in this time period and created new meaning for putting higher education in service to society. Rensselaer was a technical institute dedicated to expanding curriculum and instruction to prepare students for futures in the development of roads, bridges, and railroads through traditional classroom and laboratory methods (Boyer, 1990). Rensselaer was also a leader in alternative delivery of course work (what today would be described as extension courses or adult education) by providing classes for students in the evening and at branch locations (Brubacher and Rudy, 1997). Rensselaer was an important institution not only unto itself, but also for what it symbolized for other institutions. Engineering and technology were a developing part of the curriculum and important to the progress of the country. In response to this need, liberal arts colleges like Harvard and Yale expanded their offerings. From the perspective of service, higher education began to take note of societal needs and started to respond to these needs in ways previously absent, a tradition that continues today on many denominational college campuses.

Faculty Roles

The hallmark for professional careers in the denominational college period was the continued move toward specialization. The rapid growth and expansion of the denominational colleges contributed to the professionalization of faculty. Most colonial college faculty were tutors, although there were a few professors, but this balance was reversed in the denominational college as the number of professors increased rapidly and began to outnumber tutors. Finkelstein (1984) refers to phenomena related to the ascent of the professorial career in the early nineteenth century as the "professor movement." It was here that the shift from a largely itinerant and inexperienced workforce gave way to the beginnings of the academic career as a profession.

Higher education continued to grow and change throughout the nineteenth century. This occurred by expansion and growth on existing campuses (Yale and Harvard got bigger, for example) and growth in the number of campuses with the opening of denominational colleges and state universities. As the number and size of faculties grew, the professorship was legitimized as a long-term career (Cohen, 1998; Finkelstein, 1984).

The secularization of higher education had an impact on academic careers by expanding curriculum offerings, creating opportunities for specialization and advanced study for professors and students. More offerings in the curriculum called for a more specialized faculty. Faculty with specialized knowledge gave colleges the ability to offer advanced courses in science and mathematics. This time period also saw continued movement away from a strictly classical curriculum and toward a more practical and diverse curriculum to meet the needs of a growing country, a practice that would be solidified later in the research university. There were secular tasks to be done: training for careers other than the pulpit, providing general education for an enlightened citizenry, and passing on a shared cultural heritage that centered on American, republican values (Cohen, 1998).

By midcentury, a large number of Americans were studying in Germany and bringing ideas from the German university back to the United States. This movement created what has become known as the Germanization of higher education. These ideas included a greater emphasis on research and graduate education. These principles were not firmly rooted until century's end, but until then, the German influence did much to add professional credence to an academic career (Cohen, 1998; Cuban, 1999).

Relying on Light's (1972) conceptualization of the faculty career, Finkelstein's (1984) research examines the emergence of the modern academic role using three perspectives: the disciplinary career, the institutional career, and the external career. The external career is germane to discussions of service because it focuses on "work related activities undertaken outside the institution but rooted in a faculty member's disciplinary expertise (consulting, government service, public lecturing)" (Finkelstein, 1984, p. 8). The notion of the external career is used here as a framework for understanding how service roles evolved. (Finkelstein's work is the only source that so clearly maps the external career from 1800 to World War II. Most emphasis on the development of the faculty career starts with the emergence of the research university in the late 1800s.)

In the early 1800s, faculty were involved in external affairs, but these activities were typically not tied to their academic profession or specialization. Few faculty lectured off campus; time external to the institution was typically spent on civic and clerical affairs, such as preaching and work with missionary societies. Participation in community life typically involved holding political office or assuming leadership roles in civic associations or intellectual organizations.

Beginning in the 1850s, the external career of faculty started to shift as faculty began to exercise their expertise as educators and proponents of culture and not just proponents of religion. Faculty were starting to be involved in extrainstitutional roles as specialists and educators. A notable example is at Brown University where, in the antebellum period, a chemistry faculty member offered academic expertise in service to the state government as the head of the Rhode Island board of weights and measures. This practice of offering academic knowledge to government agencies became more firmly established in Wisconsin later in the century (Finkelstein, 1984).

Faculty involvement in civic and community affairs had always been present, but the nature of that involvement was now moving beyond religious aims. Faculty and presidents were often called on to provide direction about societal affairs and were viewed as what we would think of today as public intellectuals (Brubacher and Rudy, 1997). New responsibilities and specialization of the academic career led to a switch in service roles from those tied to religion to those tied to specialization. These evolving roles were even more firmly established with the advent of the research university.

The Research University (1860–1945)

Although federal funding for higher education was not solidified until the passing of the Morrill Act in 1862, there were earlier attempts to establish federally supported institutions. The first six U.S. presidents were in favor of some provision for a national and federally supported university, but these intentions were never fruitful (Cohen, 1998). Most notably, Washington (and later Monroe) called for a national university that focused on the primary purpose of teaching science and government. Madison lobbied Congress to establish an institution that would strengthen government. In addition, Jefferson was a champion of public-supported education, and his model for the University of Virginia, the first state university, included public support, no attachment to the church, and expansion and specialization of the curriculum (Brubacher and Rudy, 1997). A national university never materialized, but eventually state and federal support for colleges and universities did.

The passage of the Morrill Act, like nothing else before or since, created an expanded mission for higher education.

Institutional Mission

The Morrill Act, also known as the Land Grant College Act, awarded each state federal land that would be sold, with the proceeds earmarked for education in the agricultural and mechanical arts, in addition to the liberal arts (Campbell, 1998). This legislation provided for one university per state dedicated to education in the agricultural and mechanical arts. In some states, this meant starting new institutions; in others, funds were contributed to state universities already in existence.

The Morrill Act was pivotal in terms of access and curriculum because it provided publicly supported education to those for whom financial circumstances would have excluded college. In terms of curriculum, the new emphasis of the land grant college was on providing a more utilitarian education, thus attracting to higher education people who previously had attended technical institutions or did not attend higher education at all (Brubacher and Rudy, 1997). In terms of access, the act created a more open higher education system (Kerr, 1963). The act had the greatest impact on the land grant universities themselves for the funding it brought to these institutions, but it also had a profound impact on all of higher education, public and private, research and liberal arts (Kerr, 1963). Teaching, research, and service missions were firmly rooted by the founding of land grant universities, a model adopted by other sectors of higher education as well. In addition, the land grant model was influential in the overall system by focusing on making education applicable.

The land grant universities were not flooded immediately with students from all walks of life seeking education. Instead, these institutions were sustained, some barely, by the public funds they received. Public (government) support aided them during their growing pains. Had the campuses been solely reliant on student enrollment dollars to stay open, many would have closed. The funding provided by the 1862 Morrill Act allowed the universities to sustain themselves until the Morrill Act of 1890 provided an annual appropriation of federal funds that allowed these universities to face the growth of public involvement that ultimately arose (Geiger, 1999).

The Morrill Act of 1890 extended land grant funds to support African American education. Although the 1862 act did not exclude African American institutions, the cultural and political climate in the country at the time precluded the full involvement of African American students in the land grant institutions. The 1890 provisions allowed for funds to support specific institutions to teach the agricultural and mechanical arts to African American students.

The Hatch Act of 1887 extended the land grant ideal to include the creation of experimental stations that extended learning from the campus to settings in the community, particularly rural communities. Collectively, these acts established democratic ideals for education by providing applicable and accessible higher education to people on campus and in the field (Boyer, 1990; Campbell, 1998). The land grant acts and the Hatch Act (and later the Smith-Lever Act of 1914) expanded both the mission and scope of higher education. "American higher education, once devoted primarily to the intellectual and moral development of students, added *service* as a mission, and both private and public universities took up the challenge" (Boyer, 1990, p. 5). In addition to service, these acts also helped to support the research mission of these institutions. The Hatch Act provided for sites to conduct research, and the Smith-Lever Act later provided the key to linking research and dissemination by providing for the distribution of research results to those most affected (Campbell, 1998). The Smith-Lever Act was designed to help higher education disseminate information about agriculture and home economics to communities throughout each state. This act established what is known today as cooperative extension and was one of the most influential movements in placing higher education in contact with the needs of local communities (Maurrasse, 2001). Cooperative extension agents who are also faculty of land grant universities can now be found in every county throughout the United States. Cumulatively, initiatives associated with the land grant movement had a strong service orientation.

The true intersection of teaching, research, and service came together with the development of the land grant institution. The teaching component arises from extension agents and students both on campus and at the experimental stations. The acts also created expanded research opportunities, and service came into play as higher education began to meet the needs of the state through expanded educational opportunity and by addressing other needs of the public, particularly in the agricultural sector, which was very important to an economy still largely rural.

Higher education for the first time was addressing everyday problems for everyday people (Campbell, 1998). Clearly, the lasting legacy of the land grant college is service to the populace and the firm establishment of service in the triumvirate mission of higher education. The land grant movement, through its additional funding for higher education, was also instrumental in developing the university into a multiversity—a multipurpose institution inclusive of many offerings, designed to attract a diversity of students with variable interests, and an expanded mission (Kerr, 1963).

The lasting legacy of the land grant college is service to the populace and the firm establishment of service in the triumvirate mission of higher education.

Another major influence on the development of the modern American university was the adoption of the German model of higher education. The English model, with a focus on classical curriculum and undergraduate instruction, had been adopted by the colonial colleges and ultimately shaped the development of the denominational colleges. The German model of higher education focused on links between national development and research based in higher education; in addition, it established graduate education and the doctoral degree and created the framework for the disciplines that were to become the focus of scholarly attention and political power (Altbach, 1999;

Cuban, 1999; Riesman, 1980). This system was then augmented in American higher education by adding a service component that addressed the role of higher education in society (Altbach, 1999; Boyer, 1990). Ultimately, the German model would influence all aspects of American higher education, not just the research university.

The process of adopting the German model began with Professor George Ticknor at Harvard in 1825. He had studied in Germany at Göttingen and sought to bring that model to Harvard, a process that ultimately had to wait because of a lack of money and low levels of instruction. Francis Wayland at Brown and Henry Tappan at the University of Michigan in the 1850s also championed the German system (Brubacher and Rudy, 1997). But it was not until Daniel Coit Gilman founded Johns Hopkins as a research and graduate school that the German model became firmly established on American soil. Charles Eliot at Harvard followed these models and was instrumental in leading Harvard from a liberal arts college to a university by adding emphasis to graduate education and research. Eliot was also the leader in firmly establishing an elective curriculum system. This combination of the expansion of research and the elective curriculum gave birth to the modern university (Kerr, 1963).

The elective system granted students freedom in choosing their course work and granted professors the latitude to explore specializations, ultimately lending this expertise to research (Cuban, 1999; Brubacher and Rudy, 1997). From a service perspective, this development created a more responsive institution for students, one where they could study topics relevant to their developing country. The development of research at this time (1860–1900) had a service intent, especially in applied fields like agriculture and engineering. The land grant movement had paved the way for applied research in higher education, an important way for higher education to fulfill its covenant for research and knowledge with society (Boyer, 1990).

Connections between campus and government ultimately put higher education in service to the nation through the support of war efforts and global positioning, areas that would become hallmarks of the research university throughout the twentieth century. Ironically, on the contemporary campus, research, and the often myopic emphasis on it, has become one of the biggest barriers to realizing the involvement of faculty in service. The emphasis on research in the German university model, and its acceptance into the American system, firmly established the place of research in the triumvirate of higher education.

Since its place was firmly established, by around 1920, the research university has not changed markedly, and its system has had profound impacts on higher education. The nation's research universities educate a majority of the faculty who go on to teach throughout all sectors of higher education. The research university is atop the academic ladder and is a "powerful force in generating standards for the rest of higher education, chiefly by defining academic knowledge and the academic profession" (Geiger, 1999, p. 55).

One of the most relevant developments with regard to the state university and its role in service was and continues to be the Wisconsin idea. Although service was not an entirely new concept in higher education, as the tradition of higher education's relevance to society was introduced in the colonial college, developments at the University of Wisconsin from its founding in 1849 through the inauguration of President Charles Van Hise in 1903 solidified the covenant between higher education and the public (Hoeveler, 1997; Schoenfeld, 1975). As already noted, the land grant and state university movements had put higher education in service to society through changes in curriculum, access, and the translation of knowledge to practice. These ideals, like the university itself, took a while to germinate. Like all other terms possessing a moral content, the term *service* is capable of a variety of connotations according to the spirit and time of its use. In the opening of the university era (1890–1920), the meaning of *service* started to shift slightly, and the University of Wisconsin under Van Hise's leadership helped direct this movement.

The Wisconsin idea had two major components: (1) the entrance of experts (the faculty) into government to provide technical and practical expertise and (2) cooperative extension, which extended university resources, including faculty expertise, throughout the state (Curti and Carstensen, 1949; Veysey, 1965; Schoenfeld, 1975; Sellery, 1960). Although Van Hise is the person most commonly associated with the Wisconsin idea, his thinking about the university as a servant of the state developed over the years and was contributed to by John Bascom, president of University of Wisconsin from 1874 to 1887; Richard Ely, the director of the School of Economics, Political Science, and History; and John Commons, a professor in Ely's school. Collectively, these men saw the need for research conducted at the university to contribute to the state's needs (Hoeveler, 1997; Veysey, 1965).

Responding to criticisms that the University of Wisconsin "represented velvet," Van Hise championed the cause for more applied subjects and vocational courses as important factors in a liberal education. In addition, Van Hise emphasized that the university was an economic asset of the state (Pyre, 1920). The question that gripped Van Hise, and that many educators and administrators continue to grapple with today, is how far a college or university can go to promote its usefulness and so fulfill its function as an instrument of the state. The phrase "service to the commonwealth" was the rallying cry of the Van Hise administration, which created some controversy around his regime (Pyre, 1920). Nonetheless, Van Hise became known for the Wisconsin idea and for cultivating connections between the university and the state.

In the early 1900s, Wisconsin was the focus of much national interest as it stressed the utilitarian aspects of university-based agricultural research as a basis for cooperation between the university and state government (Hoeveler, 1997; Pyre, 1920; Schoenfeld, 1975; Sellery, 1960; Veysey, 1965). The university's service activities were the subject of much social comment. A book written in 1912 by D. Charles McCarthy, *The Wisconsin Idea,* and other books disseminated the Wisconsin idea throughout the states.

The Wisconsin idea pledged the University of Wisconsin to serve the state by applying its research to the solution of public problems; training experts in the physical and social sciences and joining their academic efforts to the public administrative functions of the state; and extending the work of the university, through its personnel and facilities, to the boundaries of the state (Hoeveler, 1997).

Nowhere was Van Hise's influence greater than in the area of extension. Van Hise saw direct practical service as an essential function of the university, which in Wisconsin was realized through the expansion of university extension. Originally, extension was set up to extend university influence to the state, mostly through public lectures by university faculty and staff. The work of extension at Wisconsin had somewhat broken down because university personnel were unwilling or unable to translate their work in meaningful ways for public consumption (a concern not uncommon today). Van Hise exercised leadership in this area by retaining the outreach dimension and adding new ways to prepare and distribute knowledge for immediate and practical use by the public. This practice calls for "the extension of learning, the transmutation of science into practice, the application of knowledge to concrete problems of everyday affairs" (Pyre, 1920, p. 382). The Wisconsin idea operationalized many of the tenets put forth in the land grant legislation and therefore was not limited to Wisconsin (Veysey, 1965).

The tensions that Wisconsin faced at the dawn of the twentieth century bear striking similarity to the tensions facing contemporary higher education about how to enact teaching, research, and service roles. The challenge for President Van Hise, like so many other presidents then and now, was how to effectively enact the new triumvirate of higher education, particularly in the face of opposition from those who viewed the changing nature of the university with some skepticism. A close reading of Van Hise's thinking about how best to move the University of Wisconsin forward to serve the people of Wisconsin reveals many growing pains and much negotiation of how to modernize higher education and establish traditions of excellence in teaching, research, and service (Curti and Carstensen, 1949; Pyre, 1920; Schoenfeld, 1975; Sellery, 1960; Van Hise, 1904).

The efforts of Van Hise and his contemporaries to redefine the role of the university and its faculty had a profound impact on the development of faculty roles and the professionalization of the faculty. Progressive era presidents at the turn of the twentieth century show remarkable similarity to presidents at the turn of the twenty-first century in their mutual desire to "transform the American university into a major national institution capable of meeting the needs of a rapidly changing and increasingly complex society" (Harkavy and Puckett, 1994, p. 2).

In addition to land grant institutions primarily concerned with rural interests, this time period also saw several urban grant institutions focused on the specific intent of "working to improve the quality of life in American cities experiencing the traumatic effects of industrialization, immigration, large-scale urbanization, and the unprecedented emergence of an international economy"

(Benson and Harkavy, 2000, p. 179). These campuses included Johns Hopkins in Baltimore, Columbia in New York City, and the University of Chicago.

Faculty Roles

With the rise of the American research university came the rise of academic professionalism (Rice, 1996b; Veysey, 1965). Prior to this time period, the cornerstones of traditional academic work (writing and research) were performed by people working beyond the boundaries of academe. These lay scholars did not teach and carried out their work independently (Cohen, 1998; Rice, 1996b). The expansion of the academic system to include specialization, departments, research, graduate education, funding, and rising prestige helped to make an academic career appear almost "irresistible" to lay scholars (Rice, 1996b, p. 563).

Faculty of the early research university had broken away from the liberal arts college model, which was focused almost exclusively on students and teaching, without having firmly developed a new professional persona (Cohen, 1998; Finkelstein, 1984). The German model had gained a foothold in the mid-nineteenth century, notably with the founding of Cornell University in 1869 and the graduate school at Johns Hopkins in 1876. The tenets of the German university, including professorial notions of research, academic departments, specialization, and academic freedom, took time to establish themselves. In the meantime, many graduate scholars seeking graduate-level work found their way to Germany. According to Veysey (1965), "The numerical peak of American study was reached in 1895–96, when 517 Americans were officially matriculated at German universities" (p. 130). It would be some time before these expatriate scholars and their counterparts who stayed at home would integrate research culture into the American university.

Meeting the needs of undergraduate education while developing a research culture to attract research-minded graduate students and faculty created tensions at developing research universities, tensions not unlike those found in higher education today (Clark, 1987). Along the lines of growth, there was a huge expansion in the number of faculty serving all institutions—from eleven thousand in 1880 to thirty-six thousand in 1910 (Clark, 1987). Much like faculty today, this growing body of academics faced challenges integrating their work as researchers, teachers, and public servants. The ethos of what it meant to be a faculty member, at all types of institutions, included teaching and research; the challenge was to strike a balance between these two while maintaining allegiance to society and higher education's covenant with society through new calls for faculty involvement in service.

In the research university era, the emphasis of faculty work shifted from teaching to teaching and research, with research beginning to be seen as the prime contributor to a faculty member's professional status (Clark, 1987; Cohen, 1998). As disciplines formed and solidified, departments emerged, and departmental faculty organized to contribute administration and leadership to teaching and curriculum. The founding of the American Association of University Professors (AAUP) in 1915 was an important development in the advancement of professional rights for faculty, particularly academic freedom (Geiger, 1999; Veysey, 1965).

Faculty involvement in community contexts had links with calls for academic freedom and the emergence of tenure. In several notable examples, faculty took a position on political, economic, and social issues in ways that were unpopular with administrators and trustees and had their employment terminated later. As these professors became involved in social controversy, critics within and without academe questioned the place of faculty in public discussion. Furthermore, questions arose about academic freedom and what was protected and what was not. The call for tenure emerged as an organized faculty, recognizing its collective interest and collective power, moved to protect their academic freedom (Veysey, 1965).

The emergence of tenure is germane to conversations about service because many of the faculty involved in controversial activities were acting in ways that are similar to what we could define as service today. For example, one of the activities of Professor Edward Ross, the economics professor who ultimately lost his job at Stanford over questionable activity, was organizing a public forum on capitalism (Tierney and Bensimon, 1996; Veysey, 1965). By today's standards for outreach, Ross's work in 1900 would have the potential to be counted as service, for it was tied to his expertise (economics) and designed to extend knowledge to public concerns. Controversies about the unfair dismissal of faculty for the exercise of free speech led to the creation of the AAUP

(Veysey, 1965), the group that ultimately crafted the 1940 statement of principles about tenure that would go on to be adopted by a majority of campuses throughout the country.

As the role of the faculty member as researcher became more clearly established, new types of service supplanted old notions of faculty service to the community, particularly the once-common faculty role as clergy member. By the late 1870s, the proportion of faculty involved in clerical activities had dropped to 15 percent (Finkelstein, 1984). As faculty became more specialized and as the university model evolved, public service was more firmly added to faculty responsibilities (Cohen, 1998). In fulfillment of the Wisconsin idea, faculty were called on to work with government agencies, leading to new connections between campus and state government (Veysey, 1965).

Jane Addams and her activities at the Hull-House from 1889 to 1935 also deserve mention here (Boyte, 1999; Mayfield, Hellwig, and Banks, 1999). The Hull-House was a central point for the settlement work associated with research on demographic and social characteristics of Chicago's immigrant neighborhoods. Jane Addams and her colleagues were leaders in establishing the field of social work and the sociological methods that would become affiliated with the Chicago school of sociology into the 1930s. The relationship between the Hull-House residents and the University of Chicago sociologists (including George Herbert Mead) created a tradition of studying the city and its inhabitants and of linking social reform and social science (Harkavy and Puckett, 1993). Ironically, the socially progressive work of the Hull-House gave way to more aloof and socially disconnected research that is often the subject of criticism in today's research universities.

The 1890s to the late 1910s mirrored the American university's transition from an outwardly directed, service-oriented institution to an inwardly directed, discipline-centered institution. It was also a marker of the separation of knowledge production from knowledge use, indeed, of social science from social reform, by the end of the progressive era (Harkavy and Puckett, 1994, p. 4).

With increased specialization came the growth of disciplinary associations, many of which, particularly in the social sciences, placed public service on their agendas (Cohen, 1998). Associations were a link between the work of the academy and the general public. The trend started early in the twentieth century, with faculty serving state governments. As faculty expertise developed and national need arose, faculty moved into positions of federal service and were instrumental in research and development activities that would become very important in World War II (Finkelstein, 1984). Collectively and cumulatively, what emerged for faculty were specialization, increased visibility of expertise, academic freedom, disciplinary associations, academic departments, and academic rank (Cohen, 1998; Finkelstein, 1984). Faculty lives in the fully developed research university bore little resemblance to the lives of their counterparts sixty years earlier and a fair resemblance to the lives of their counterparts sixty years later.

By the end of World War II, the components of the academic role had clearly emerged and crystallized into the highly differentiated model by which we recognize the professor today: teaching, research, student advisement, administration, and institutional and public service. Since its crystallization, the model has shown remarkable durability; over thirty-five years and enormous fluctuations in the fortunes of American higher education, it has come to approach even more closely its ideal typical expression through greater emphasis on research activity, fuller participation in academic citizenship, and fuller development of the public role (Finkelstein, 1984).

Mass Education (1945–1975)

Cohen (1998) calls the mass higher education era the golden age of higher education. It was a time when higher education enjoyed massive growth in enrollments, financial support, and diversification of institutional types, with the focus shifting from education for the elite to education for the masses (Geiger, 1999).

Institutional Mission
Changes introduced by the founding of research universities accelerated at unprecedented rates with expansions in curriculum offerings and access. The service mission of higher education most prevalent for this period is evident in how teaching and research roles expanded. In this time period, "universities and the nation had joined in common cause" (Boyer, 1990, p. 10) to support national research and educational needs.

This time period is marked by the expansion and diversification of the student body (and the faculty) as new opportunities arose for students of diverse socioeconomic classes, races, ages, abilities, and gender. Offerings expanded in terms of outreach to the public, with courses at branch locations, through correspondence, and through extension courses to meet specialized training needs, which were not necessarily offered for credit. Continuing-education units provided an interface for higher education and the many new communities it was serving. All of these educational trends created a post-secondary system more responsive to student and general public needs. Furthermore, given trends in diversification, higher education was closer to the people and more in touch with responding to their needs.

One of the legacies of the Land Grant Act was, and remains, expanded access to higher education for people who had not previously been involved. The nineteenth-century student body, though expanded by the Morrill Act, was still fairly homogeneous: white, mostly male, either elite or of the expanding middle class. Although more open than before, higher education still eluded and excluded the majority of American people. This started to change rapidly with the end of World War II and the massive movement of former soldiers into higher education.

The Servicemen's Readjustment Act of 1944 (the GI Bill) was passed by Congress as a way for the nation to adapt to the wave of service men and women who were returning home from war. The GI Bill provided many benefits to soldiers participating in higher education, including unemployment insurance, counseling services, medical care, tuition, book expenses, and living expenses (Brubacher and Rudy, 1997; Cohen, 1998). This legislation rapidly changed the face and complexion of American higher education. Campuses were deluged with students, many of whom were different from the higher education students of years before. These new students were older, had families, and had had significant life experiences.

In addition to the GI Bill, advances in civil rights also changed the face of higher education (Cohen, 1998). The Morrill Act of 1890 had created a separate higher education system for African American students. The groundbreaking legal case of *Brown* v. *Board of Education* in 1954 ruled that separate educational opportunities were inherently unequal. This decision was extended to higher education in the case of *Florida ex rel. Hawkins* v. *Board of Control* in 1956. These cases put racial equity on the minds of the American people and administrators in higher education.

The step for equality in education came by way of the Civil Rights Act of 1964, which supported higher education in its integration efforts. To be certain, integration did not come quickly or easily regardless of legislation, and the struggle for diversity and equality persists even today. The racial integration of higher education changed the makeup of colleges and universities. Title IX legislation supported integration on the basis of gender. Expanded federal support of and involvement in higher education shifted thinking about a college education from a private to a public good. From a service standpoint, the expansion of student populations with respect to diversity and sheer numbers forced and allowed the education system to focus more on serving the needs of students. Furthermore, the expansion and democratization of student populations eventually led to calls for more relevant curriculum to address the needs of students and society.

World War II also had a profound impact on higher education in the area of research. The connections that had been established between universities and the government during the development of land grant and research universities flourished under the demands of the war effort. Academics as researchers were called on to support the nation's global economic position and the expansion of the defense establishment. As academics began to staff agencies in Washington, their influence and expertise helped to channel significant federal funding into higher education (Boyer, 1990).

Partnerships between higher education and the federal government ensued, with the protection of American national interest and international influence as primary goals. These partnerships forced universities to focus increasingly on research directly relevant to the needs of the federal government and consequently left less attention and support for more esoteric (and hence less applied) research. The land grant movement had created partnerships between government and higher education to produce knowledge for the common good; wartime and postwar funding expanded these partnerships and their influence on the focus and direction of the campuses. "American universities [had] been changed almost as much by the federal research grant as by the land grant idea" (Kerr, 1963, p. 49).

Colleges and universities in the mass education era underwent some revolutionary changes that created a new relationship between higher education and society. The increased number and diversity of students attending colleges and universities placed higher education in the public mind, and outreach changes, including extension and adult and lifetime learning, brought the university in contact with students who might never before have thought of attending traditional college courses. As higher education claimed a higher profile in the public eye, the campus became a center for educational advancement and cultural life. The GI Bill and federal loan programs, combined with the expansion of the higher education system, led to new notions of a college education. Higher education, once seen as a privilege reserved primarily for the middle and upper classes, came to be seen as a citizen's right (Boyer, 1990).

During this time the number of community colleges expanded. As a primary educational mission, community colleges were focused on providing access to new populations of nontraditional and first-generation college students. The service function of these institutions was embedded in missions of open access and curriculum tied to transfer, remediation, and workforce preparation functions (Cohen, 1995; Stanton, Giles, and Cruz, 1999).

Faculty Roles
By the mid-1940s, the academic profession was marked by professionalization and specialized faculty expertise, bringing about visibility for faculty and increases in faculty salaries (Finkelstein, 1984). As higher education experienced massive expansion and diversification, the number of people entering academic careers increased. The demographics of the faculty also started to shift as more women entered the profession (around 33 percent by 1975). As the higher education system grew, hierarchical relations formed among institutions, with research universities at the helm and community colleges perceived as being less prestigious. Hierarchies also emerged within the disciplines, as the hard sciences, those more inclined to research (including grant funding), came to be seen as models that the soft or social sciences would seek

(and be pressured) to emulate (Clark, 1987). These hierarchies would lead to increased tensions between teaching, research, and service and the relative importance of each, depending on institutional type and discipline.

Faculty status was viewed along similar lines. With the surging enrollments of this period and the subsequent need to hire faculty, the average age of faculty members declined (Cohen, 1998). The advent of affirmative action forced institutions to draw up affirmative action plans, which then contributed to diversity in faculty hiring, although this increased diversity was slow to arrive and varied greatly by institutional type and department. Typically, the more highly ranked a department was, the fewer women and minorities were present, a situation that continues today.

The mass education era was one of extremes. The outset saw fat times for higher education: faculty numbers were expanding, as were student enrollments. The public trust in higher education was high. Faculty were valued for their specialized knowledge and the contributions they could make to society. But by the end of this era, funding for higher education started to decline and shifts began to take place in how higher education functioned. There was an increased emphasis on the differences between faculty and administrators and an increased sense of bureaucracy in colleges and universities. To protect their rights and working conditions, faculty started to unionize (Cohen, 1998).

Diversification and expansion of higher education also meant confusion over the roles of faculty members. In 1958, Theodore Caplow and Reece McGee defined this new reality when they observed that while young faculty were hired as teachers, they were evaluated primarily as researchers. This stands in contrast to what it meant to be a faculty member before World War II, when faculty were hired and promoted on the basis of their role as teacher-scholar (Rice, 1996b). A teacher-scholar faculty member was typically employed at a liberal arts college and was widely respected as a scholar whose research efforts helped to promote student learning. The emphasis was on the internal teaching role. The teacher-scholar model of the faculty member gave way to a more research-focused image as higher education changed in the 1950s (Rice, 1996b). With these changes, "scholarship became research, and teaching and research became activities that competed for faculty members' time" (cited in Rice, 1996b, p. 564). Although the notion of what it meant to be a professor was tied to teaching, research emerged as a more prevalent form of scholarship (Cohen, 1998; Fairweather, 1996, 2002). This shift created a somewhat dichotomous and tense relationship between what it meant to be a teacher and what it meant to be a researcher, a legacy that remains in higher education today (Fairweather, 2002). Although both are important dimensions to the definition of a faculty member, given promotion and tenure standards in higher education that value research over teaching, the professoriat was becoming more focused on research (Fairweather, 1996). The emphasis on research over other aspects of faculty roles changed the focus of faculty work away from local concerns of teaching toward more global ones of research (Clark, 1987; Kerr, 1963; Rice, 1996b).

> **The emphasis on research over other aspects of faculty roles changed the focus of faculty work away from local concerns of teaching toward more global ones of research.**

The opening of higher education to greater numbers of students, who were more diverse in terms of age, race, and gender, also meant changes in classroom practices. The 1960s saw increased interest in experiential learning and the need to connect classroom experiences with those beyond the classroom (Kolb, 1984; McDaniels, 2002). As higher education became more open to diverse students, faculty needed to respond to these students through curriculum and pedagogy.

Boyer (1990) observes, "Ironically, at the very time America's higher education institutions were becoming more open and inclusive, the culture of the professoriate was becoming more hierarchical and restrictive" (pp. 12–13). That is, higher education became more bureaucratic and more concerned with matters of prestige, particularly in research universities. Perhaps this is the crux of what has become the focal point of much of the criticism facing higher education today. The federal funding of higher education that became prevalent in this era created what was essentially a federal grant university (Kerr, 1963) that put professorial focus more directly on research, with much less attention granted to teaching and service (Cuban, 1999).

Although the work norms of faculty at research universities are not necessarily representative of all faculty, the research university is often a leader in terms of trends that shape all of higher education. Trends in research universities often trickle down to other campuses (Morphew, 2002). The net result for faculty of these developments meant a disgruntled public that viewed faculty as overly focused on their own individual work, with not enough attention directed to the education of students for productive lives in society.

The Contemporary Era (1975–present)

During the mass education era, American higher education expanded in both size and scope and became firmly established as one of the leading institutions in American society. Throughout the contemporary era, defined here as 1975 to the present, the expansion has slowed, and the higher education system has begun to face challenges and criticisms of its higher profile.

Institutional Mission

The contemporary era has seen colleges and universities face criticism of their actions and outlooks, while higher education is called on to meet new challenges and revisit old tasks in new ways. Higher education increasingly has to do more with less, while answering to a critical audience of students and the larger public.

The research climate that was a major force in the growth of the higher education system during the mass education era has also been responsible for generating much of the criticism leveled against higher education today. Research missions, which have driven funding and expansion of the education system, with particular influence on the development of the nation's research universities, have also cast their shadows across the function of all higher education (Boyer, 1990; Cuban, 1999). Institutions value research contributions, which generate funds for individual and departmental scholarly activity. As state support for higher education has fallen (the result of many factors, including the legacy of tax cuts in the 1980s), higher education institutions have become more reliant on external (research) funds and have placed more emphasis on securing external funding. Research funds help fill gaps in government funding.

Another result of dwindling government support has been tuition increases. As the cost of a degree has risen, so too has public scrutiny of the higher education system. When students, parents, and community members review the education system, they see faculty members focused more firmly on research than teaching (Cuban, 1999). The faculty become pinned between conflicting expectations: their constituents want to see them focused on teaching and students, while their administrators want to see them promoting the university through their achievements and, not inconsequentially, securing grants and external funding to support their work and the university.

The contemporary era is a time of continued growth in both the number of students and the number of institutions, although the rate of growth slowed from the mass education era (Cohen, 1998). At the dawn of the twenty-first century, there are over thirty-seven hundred colleges and universities offering and awarding degrees at the associate and bachelor's levels. In addition, more than six thousand institutions, ranging from proprietary schools to organizations offering occupationally related graduate degrees, provide other forms of postsecondary education (Cohen, 1998). The higher education system is incredibly diverse, with public and private research, comprehensive, liberal arts, and community colleges. Higher education is more accessible than ever before; interested individuals can tap into all types of higher education for degrees, credentials, or curiosity, on campus and off. The infusion of technology on campus has extended access to education and information to levels unimaginable at the start of the contemporary era; through technology, for example, students in New Jersey can share virtual classrooms with students from Kenya.

A host of other issues face higher education today, including the purpose of a college education in contemporary society. One aspect of these discussions concerns "curricular vocationalism" (Altbach, 1999, p. 26), whereby students demand more focus on job preparation, to better find jobs and earn a living. Proponents of this outlook are interested less in the traditional goals of a liberal education—critical thinking, appreciation for literature, art, culture, creating a well-rounded individual—and more in the practical matters of securing work. A related issue involves expanded links between higher education and industry that have put pressure on higher education to incorporate needed skills into the curriculum. This focus on practical skills and training can create conflict, particularly in liberal arts institutions. Faculty who attempt to stand by what they see as the traditional role of the university and the professor—

intellectual work, promoting the life of the mind—come in for criticism that they are not responding to changing social conditions and the needs of the public.

As higher education has expanded its offerings and its clientele while watching its governmental revenues dwindle, the need to attract and retain students at any particular institution has grown. One result has been what might be called a consumerist vision of the higher education system, which differs in many ways from previous visions of higher education. In previous eras, colleges and other institutions offered their courses for the good of the student and the society, but without particular input from outside interests. Even into the mass education era, when students were gaining influence, students by and large accepted the education they were offered. Today, however, higher education, and particularly a degree or other credential, is increasingly viewed by students, parents, and the general public ("consumers") as a "good" for which they pay, and teaching is hence seen as a "service" provided. This vision of the higher education enterprise has put additional pressure on the "service providers": institutions and their faculties. If the service desired is not offered, then the consumers (the students) complain and begin to look elsewhere to meet their needs.

The tension between the particular interests of faculty and the broader interests of higher education's institutions, which perhaps invariably conflict to some degree, may well be intensifying. This may be a consequence of an increasingly managerial culture of higher education, focused on administrative task and management, similar to common school administration (Clark, 1987). This managerial culture contrasts with a collegial culture based on research and peer review (Burgan, 1998; Carlisle and Miller, 1998). In the former culture, advancement is achieved through training in administration; in the latter, it is achieved through education and socialization in the disciplines (Rice, 1996b). Although these concepts do not need to stand in opposition to one another, in a time of increasing demands and shrinking resources, the focus of faculty

The tension between the particular interests of faculty and the broader interests of higher education's institutions may well be intensifying.

work has become knowledge that is economically useful and applied (managerial culture) and not knowledge as an end in itself (collegial culture). On many campuses, this translates to a business culture of higher education where students are clients, consumers, and customers who need to be pleased and offered an education with a guarantee of employment, success, and wealth. Preparation for broadened civic life can stand in conflict with the desire for an education to expediently prepare students for the workforce.

Higher education in America today is a diverse and massive enterprise. Any institution so broad-reaching, attempting to do so many things for so many different people, may find itself at odds internally (Kerr, 1963). As higher education diversifies demographically and institutionally, it makes its way into the homes of more Americans, creating both more awareness of higher education and more concern about what it does and does not do and at what cost. Unfortunately, higher education lacks public support because governments are reluctant to increase spending.

In a nutshell, what faces higher education is concern about what academe does and for whom, and at what cost. There is little understanding of what higher education does because historically, the academy has been an internally focused and autonomous organization (Altbach, 1995). If the higher education system is to reclaim the attention and support of the American people, more responsive institutions, which pay attention to calls for accountability and responsiveness, are needed (Chaffee, 1997, 1998). Colleges and universities are "social institutions embedded in the wider society and subject to society's constraining forces" (Berdahl, Altbach, and Gumport, 1999b, p. 1):

> Universities—and by extension many four-year and two-year postsecondary institutions—have generally had ambivalent relations with their surrounding societies—both involved and withdrawn, both servicing and criticizing, both needing and being needed. Eric Ashby identified the central dilemma of this ambivalence: a university "must be sufficiently stable to sustain the ideal which gave it birth and sufficiently responsive to remain relevant to the society which supports it" [Berdahl and others, 1999b, p. 4].

A major movement in contemporary higher education is centered around service and engagement as a way to respond to many of these criticisms and as a means to express to higher education's multiple publics (including parents, legislators, and students) what higher education does and how it contributes to society. Campuses present a huge intellectual and human resource for local communities, and there are many contemporary calls for greater involvement as a means to link communities with their campuses (Checkoway, 1997). One societal factor—the declining percentage of citizens participating in civic affairs—has shifted attention to the civic role of higher education, with particular focus on higher education's role in preparing citizens for civic roles (Astin, 1994; Cohen, 1995; Edgerton, 1995a; Putnam, 1996; Boyte and Farr, 2000). Many colleges and universities are invigorating or initiating character education, civics, and service-learning programs in response to concerns about lack of participation in democratic processes.

Most campuses include the development of responsible citizens in their mission statements, but there is concern among the general public that this mission is not being met:

> *The general public is seeking greater engagement with social issues from the academy, demanding that higher education better prepare the young for work, frame research agendas in ways that address social ills, and do away with the traditional attitude of noblesse oblige toward community service. Land grant institutions, in particular, were formed to serve these values directly. Being useful to society was a primary reason for their existence. But during the past half-century the research university has become a more exclusive professional organization, with peer-reviewed research productivity dominating its culture. Knowledge, solely or primarily for its own sake, has become a primary justification for faculty investment. Research productivity, as defined by the number of peer-reviewed journal articles and books published, is often the criterion of success. Thus, the academy turned inward for its character and sense of worth and being. Its separation from society has been conscious, deliberate, and defining* [Braskamp and Wergin, 1998, pp. 79–80].

Current attention to civic, democratic, and leadership education in addition to service-learning and citizenship preparation points to the need to address these concerns (Jacoby, 1996). There have been several approaches based on institutional type addressing the call for service. For example, the Council of Independent Colleges has been active throughout the past decade in its work to expand the unique missions of liberal arts colleges and their civic, regional, and religious focus and how these tie to civic engagement.

Any conversation about contemporary higher education and institutional approaches to service must take place cognizant of differences in institutional type. Stanton, Giles, and Cruz (1999) provide a useful framework to examine these differences from the perspective of institutional responses to service (see Table 1). Based on factors like mission, location, history, and student population, campuses can have variable approaches to service and engagement.

TABLE 1
A Typology of Institutional Responses to Service

Type	Primary Educational Mission	Definition of Service
Liberal arts college	Citizenship training for democracy	Engaging with ideas of value
	Character formation	Training citizens for public life
Research university	Expanding the knowledge base	Applying knowledge to solve social problems
Professional school	Teaching applied, concrete skills	Training professionals to perform needed social functions
		Clinical training
Community college	Providing access to nontraditional populations	Access to educational opportunity
		Access to employment opportunity

Faculty Roles

Because faculty are the focus of much of the criticism leveled at higher education and because faculty roles are such a large part of the operation of higher education, an exploration of contemporary faculty roles, particularly service roles, is necessary.

The 1970s saw the entrance of a new cohort of faculty to higher education, who, unlike their counterparts from the 1950s, were research oriented and more truly teacher-scholars (Cuban, 1999; Finkelstein, 1984; Finkelstein, Seal, and Schuster, 1998; Rice, 1996b). The late 1990s and early 2000s are giving way to yet another academic generation that is influencing the professorial landscape in many and new ways. The expansion of the professoriat from the 1950s to the 1970s has given way to a wave of retirements and new hiring beginning in the 1980s. Replacing the graying professoriat has led to faculties across all sectors where no less than 30 percent of faculty are new (Finkelstein and others, 1998), and this new cohort of faculty is increasingly more diverse than the professors they are replacing.

In 1969, 47 percent of all full-time faculty were employed at universities, 39 percent at other four-year colleges, and 15 percent at community colleges (Finkelstein, Seal, and Schuster, 1998). Based on analysis of the faculty from the National Survey of Postsecondary Faculty database from 1993, those figures point to slight shifts in where faculty work. Doctorate-granting universities house 44.8 percent of the nation's faculty. Comprehensive universities account for 23.2 percent of faculty, liberal arts colleges for only 7.4 percent, and public two-year colleges 19.3 percent. This new generation of faculty is diverse with regard to gender and minority status. The faculty is increasingly international and holds appointments outside the traditionally liberal arts fields (Finkelstein, Seal, and Schuster, 1998). Roughly 75 percent of all faculty are employed in public universities (Clark, 1987). Among today's faculty, there is also much diversity with regard to rank. In response to budget pressures, many campuses are relying on part-time and adjunct faculty to fulfill teaching roles. This change in the makeup of the faculty has interesting impacts on faculty service, with adjunct and part-time faculty being more inclined to participate in community outreach initiatives (Antonio, Astin, and

Cress, 2000) and fewer full-time professors available to support internal service obligations.

In addition to their diversity, another interesting fact about these new faculty members is their orientation and the pressures they face. The research about faculty is clear that there is a strong emphasis on research at all levels (Cuban, 1999; Fairweather, 1996, 2002). Even at liberal arts colleges, where faculty have traditionally been seen as teachers first and foremost, faculty find they cannot get tenure without publishing (Boyer, 1990; Fairweather, 1996). New faculty face increasingly demanding standards for promotion and tenure as expectations for hours in the classroom and for engagement in research activity increase. Furthermore, in the light of calls for accountability and for better representing higher education to society, faculty are also increasingly engaged in activities focused on external communications. One of the major debates within the academic profession today concerns the appropriate balance of teaching, research, and service (Altbach, 1995; Fairweather, 2002). This debate relates not only to the profession but also to the role of higher education.

Faculty roles have also shifted with the advent of technology and other classroom innovations. Technology simplifies communication with colleagues nationally and allows additional contact options with students. Some campuses face pressures for expanding on-line learning options for students, as well as continued expansion of experiential learning opportunities in the classroom. Service-learning, in particular, has seen a renaissance in the 1990s and into the 2000s as campuses seek ways to involve students more fully in civic life (Boyte, 1999; Jacoby, 1996; Boyte and Farr, 2000; McDaniels, 2002). Along with the calls for expanded approaches to teaching and learning (including service-learning), faculty face pressure to offer students degrees in truncated periods of time, creating pressures between breadth and depth of study.

> **One thing is certain: the academic profession needs to represent itself more effectively to external constituencies.**

One thing is certain: the academic profession needs to represent itself more effectively to external constituencies (Chaffee, 1997, 1998). Following are just some of the contemporary thoughts about faculty and the social perception of them:

> *On the whole, the faculty of the 1990s have become more and more accustomed to hearing themselves characterized as part of the problem, as a central feature of the academy that needs to be "fixed" if the higher education enterprise is to maintain viability (and market share) in the coming era [Finkelstein, Seal, and Schuster, 1998, pp. 2–3].*

> *We [faculty] are told we need to do a better job of assessing our students, for example; increasingly, faculty are expected to do less of what they have come to think of as central to their role—research—and more of what they often do not know how to do—serve the larger society [Tierney, 1998, p. 2].*

Faculty today are required to do more with less: to prepare students for the workforce *and* for greater involvement in civic life, to make faculty work responsive to societal needs *and* to be accountable to public demands for greater faculty productivity. How can academics respond to all these demands, criticisms, and challenges facing higher education? The work of faculty, as teachers, researchers, and service providers, is pivotal to realizing campus missions for engagement. A conscious and coordinated effort on behalf of faculty and administration is needed to reclaim the outreach mission that holds such a prominent place in the history of higher education in America. This is at the heart of creating the engaged campus: an endeavor that calls for higher education to look inward to assess its resources and then to extend these resources to meet the needs of the community.

Conclusion

Analysis of these eras from a service perspective leads to the following observations and conclusions. The colonial college was "in service" to the public in a very limited way, for a small number of privileged students had access to higher education. Nonetheless, society benefited by introduction to the value of higher education and by expanding a learned society that had a prominent role in leading the colonies to self-determination and the American Revolution.

The denominational college era shifted this orientation because higher education had become more prevalent and accessible. Even those lacking a higher education themselves saw the cultural, educational, social, and economic benefits of a college education. This positive outlook on higher education was in part forged through the college and community alliances that were formed to attract higher education to communities of the new West and to attract students to these institutions.

The research university era perhaps more than any other time in history solidified the explicitly public service mission of higher education. The land grant movement legislated and solidified relationships based on service between higher education and the public. The service was no longer limited to educating students (although that was still part of it), but also put higher education in service to states through supporting agricultural development and providing technical expertise to the expanding nation. This time period firmly established the triumvirate mission of teaching, research, and service so commonly held in higher education today.

The contemporary era could also be called the postresearch university era. Clearly, the research university is a central player in the educational system, but it is only one player. The contemporary system is diversified beyond historical expectation and is working to respond to public criticism of higher education. The service aspect of this period is characterized by engagement as colleges and universities throughout the country seek to recoup the public trust by engaging with their communities. Higher education is in the midst of reacting to and hopefully recovering from public criticism of waste and isolation. Engagement, unlike service, connotes reciprocal relationships and transcends teaching, research, and service. The contemporary era sees service reformulated as engagement as a means to regain the public trust.

For higher education to represent itself to external constituencies adequately, it is vital for the work of its faculty to be clearly articulated and for colleges and universities to function effectively. Faculty service has both external and internal aspects. These are the subjects of the next two chapters.

Internal Service: Faculty at Work as Institutional and Disciplinary Citizens

IN MODERN ACADEMIC LIFE, service takes up much of a faculty member's time. While the idealized scholar spends time gathering data, poring over journals in conducting research, writing drafts to synthesize new insights, preparing lectures, and educating students with pithy phrases or oratorical flourishes, wry anecdotes, or germane examples, the faculty member actually spends considerable time sitting in committee meetings, answering e-mail queries from students and colleagues, scheduling lecture series and conferences, reviewing articles for journals, and advising student groups. This second group of activities, which falls under the rubric of service to the discipline and campus, are part of the hidden curriculum of faculty life.

Service is ever-present and often unrecognized as an important part of faculty work. Service activities are likely to go unrewarded (Boice, 2000). When professors are evaluated for retention, promotion, or tenure, the standards by which they are judged are often explicit regarding research productivity: presentations, a certain number of publications in journals of a certain standing, a certain number (or amount) of grants procured, a book, and so forth. Standards for the evaluation of teaching tend to be less explicit, but teaching loads, evaluations, and criticisms offer quantitative comparisons for departments that seek them, and typically institutions have specific means to evaluate teaching. Service, however, is difficult to quantify, and faculty members often receive little departmental direction when considering service loads (Bensimon, Ward, and Sanders, 2000;

> **Service is ever-present and often unrecognized as an important part of faculty work.**

Boice, 2000). Furthermore, the outcomes and effectiveness of faculty service are often unknown; sometimes there are immediate results of service efforts (such as new general education requirements) but the long-term impact (the relationship of these new requirements to student learning) is usually unknown and unknowable (Austin and Gamson, 1983).

In the light of current concerns about faculty work and calls for engagement with communities, there has been increased attention to the terminology used to capture the essence of what faculty do as service providers (Boyer, 1990; Crosson, 1983; Fear and Sandmann, 1995; Lynton, 1995; Rice, 1996a; Elman and Smock, 1985). In contrast to other aspects of faculty work, *service* is a word with multiple meanings for faculty:

> *The word "teaching" conjures up mental images of students, faculty and syllabi. The word "research" suggests journal articles, reports, and/ or laboratories. This is true despite the fact that technology is greatly changing the teaching and learning process and new epistemologies such as action research are changing the face of research. However, the words "faculty professional service," do not yet command a uniform image, but rather a mix match of images that vary from faculty directing girl scout troops to developing an intake evaluation for a local homeless shelter* [O'Meara, 1997, p. 6].

On some campuses, the service role of faculty has come to mean institutional, campus, or disciplinary citizenship, or what I refer to in this monograph as *internal service* and Fear and Sandmann (1995) call *inreach*. In their definition of inreach, Fear and Sandmann include "activities associated with generating, transmitting, applying and/or preserving knowledge for the benefit of audiences *internal* to the university" (p. 117). My expansion of the term *inreach* to *internal service* includes the departmental and university service and citizenship activities that Fear and Sandmann discussed, but it also encompasses similar activities at the disciplinary level, such as service to national and regional associations and conference activities. Fear and Sandmann indicate that distinguishing internal service (that is, inreach) from external service (that is, outreach) is important in any discussion of academic service, because the audience for internal service, which typically includes other faculty and administrators, generally tends to be familiar with the requirements of faculty service. External audiences, in contrast, are usually less familiar with the service demands of faculty life, particularly service to the department, college, and discipline (that is, internal service).

The inclusion of internal service roles in a monograph largely tied to the theme of engagement warrants comment. In the light of calls for engaged campuses, faculty service roles and their clarification are important. Thus, it is necessary to clarify the internal and external roles of service distinctly, for too often these definitions of service are combined into ambiguity and irrelevance. By defining all faculty service roles, internal and external, my intent is to bring meaning to the importance of both of these aspects of the service component of faculty work. Furthermore, if institutions are to engage in meaningful ways with their external audiences, they must first function effectively internally. It is faculty involvement in internal service roles that contributes to and helps create institutional and disciplinary fitness (Berberet, 1999; Wong and Tierney, 2001; McMillin and Berberet, 2002).

This chapter provides an overview of faculty service roles on campus and within disciplines and presents examples of how the internal service aspect of faculty work is communicated and rewarded in higher education. The chapter concludes with an overview of how different variables such as race, gender, and institutional type relate to internal service roles.

Service to the Campus

In early American higher education, faculty members tended to be generalists, able and willing to teach across the curriculum, which was, admittedly, rather narrow, concentrating on the classics. The university was led by a president, and faculty involvement in what today would be considered institutional affairs was limited. Organizational structures were flat and decision making rather straightforward. This changed with the evolution of the disciplines and the emergence of faculty specialization (Clark, 1987; Cohen, 1998; Finkelstein, 1984). As the higher education system evolved, faculty began to claim academic and scholarly specialties. In time, these specialists, whose numbers grew as the number of students increased, began to form cadres of specialists within the university structures, the beginnings what would become the academic department.

As faculty specialized and departments grew, it became more difficult for a president to understand and govern the actions of individual faculty members. Administrative layers developed, beginning with departmental administration (Veysey, 1965). It was easier for a department chair to oversee the work of a specialist in his (or, rarely, her) department than for the university president to do so. As departments became increasingly specialized, faculty service in support of the area of specialization (the discipline or department) became increasingly important, especially in areas tied directly to that expertise, most notably matters of curriculum (Cohen, 1998).

Shared governance is a cornerstone of faculty service. It suggests that the president and administration, the faculty, and students share responsibility for the management of a campus:

> *The president and administration must attend to the planning and direction of operations as well as the representation of the institution to its various constituents—inside and outside its walls. The faculty must attend not only to the fostering of teaching and research but also to their structures in programs and curricula. The share for students was encouraged "within the limits of attainable effectiveness"* [Burgan, 1998, p. 16].

This shared view of governance distributes power for university decision making among the faculty, administrators, and other constituencies (Eckel, 2000a; Miller, 1996). While administrators rely on faculty input for issues ranging from general education requirements to student conduct, the general foundation for shared governance is that faculty authority emanates from disciplinary specialization.

Faculty members serve their institutions in many ways beyond their roles as teachers and researchers. Faculty acting in these roles are sometimes referred to as academic or institutional citizens (Burgan, 1998; Fear and Sandmann,

1995). Finsen (2002) identifies three areas of institutional citizenship (that is, internal campus service):

Academic oversight: Faculty service that supports the academic mission of the campus and is tied to faculty expertise. Without faculty contributions in these areas, the academic mission of the campus would suffer. Examples are program review or accreditation, general education, academic advising, faculty evaluation, and academic appeals.

Institutional governance: Faculty support institutional governance roles through decision-making responsibilities that support the campus at the institutional level. Examples are budget oversight, strategic planning, campus assessment, administrative hiring, and mission and goal oversight.

Institutional support: Service in this area supports the overall building and maintenance of campus life and is not tied to faculty disciplinary expertise. Examples are parking, student recruitment, alumni relations, and the cultural arts.

Faculty members typically enact their institutional citizenship in these areas by participating in committee meetings, writing reports, and helping make decisions.

In addition, faculty acting in certain administrative and quasi-administrative capacities are doing so as part of service (Berberet, 2002). Administrative service occurs when faculty contribute to some aspect of departmental or unit functioning. For example, an English professor coordinating graduate programs would be doing administrative (or at least quasi-administrative) service. Department chairs, though making an important contribution to departmental functioning, are not doing so in the name of service. They are paid to chair the department, and this work is their primary role. In contrast, the faculty member who coordinates a particular graduate program within a department is still maintaining faculty duties and is doing the coordination only as a service to the department. A coordination role may carry with it a small stipend or course release and would be characterized as administrative service instead of part of a position, because the primary identification of the person is still faculty member rather than administrator. Departments rely on faculty service—administrative and otherwise—to realize their mission and support the smooth operation of the department. Service engages faculty in the inner workings of the campus or department. Faculty involvement in governance of the university is a cornerstone of higher education and faculty work (Austin and Gamson, 1983; Kennedy, 1997; Miller, 1996; Miller, Vacik, and Benton, 1998).

Faculty involvement in departmental service is key to departmental functioning, and departmental committees are often where faculty spend much of their service time. Departments rely on their faculty to make curricular decisions, admit students, decide on scholarships, and perform other service as required to help the department function smoothly. The level of service required in a department depends on the size of the department and type of institution. Typically, in larger departments, each individual faculty member sees less service involvement because there are more faculty to cover departmental and institutional tasks (Austin and Gamson, 1983).

Higher education has become notoriously bureaucratic. Some argue that faculty power is minimized by an increasingly managerial culture that exists in colleges and universities (Altbach, 1995; Burgan, 1998; Leatherman, 1998). Faculty involvement in shared governance and institutional decision making is at a crossroads. In one direction is an expanded mid- and senior-level administration, leaving faculty with limited power in meaningful institutional affairs. In the other direction is the need for faculty to maintain involvement in institutional affairs as a way to shape campus futures and realize institutional missions (Finsen, 2002). Institutions still rely heavily on faculty decision making in areas ranging from admissions and curricular decisions at the departmental level to decisions about parking and performing arts at the institutional level. It is crucial for faculty to embrace their roles as institutional and academic citizens to preserve the values that have shaped the academic profession and to support campus missions (Berberet, 1999, 2002; Burgan, 1998).

Service to the Discipline

In addition to their involvement with departmental service, faculty members also serve their disciplines. Disciplinary and professional associations come together to offer colleagueship for faculty with common disciplinary interests (for example, the American Psychological Association) and for faculty from different disciplines with common educational interests (for example, the American Association for Higher Education Forum on Faculty Roles and Rewards). The number of associations is staggering, and it seems that every discipline and subspecialty is represented by an association. Each association has some administrative overhead, but for the most part, these associations rely on the faculty members that comprise them for the expertise and service that drive the associations.

Disciplinary service takes many forms. Associations, like departments, are often decentralized and rely on committees to conduct much of their work. An active and involved scholar can easily find herself wearing service hats in a variety of associations: membership committees, program committees, and reward committees, for example. In addition, most associations have newsletters and journals, which are often written, edited, and reviewed through the service of the membership.

These activities are rarely rewarded monetarily. They do look good on a vita, but an overinvolvement in disciplinary service can easily distract a junior faculty member from his or her research agenda, which usually weighs more heavily when achievements are reviewed (Berberet, 2002; Burgan, 1998; Fairweather, 1996). For many scholars, the greatest benefits of disciplinary service are recognition and connection with and among other scholars in one's discipline. These networking benefits may well outweigh the drawbacks of unpaid, underrewarded disciplinary service (Boice, 2000).

The discipline is the dominant force in the working lives of most faculty members; it provides a foundation for faculty expertise in the classroom and in research. Disciplinary specialty and institutional locations make up the similarities and differences among American professors (Clark, 1983, 1987). The term *colleague* has multiple definitions for scholars, as a professor may have more in common with peers at the national or regional level than with fellow faculty at the campus level. Math professors at Michigan State University, for example, tend to have more in common with math professors at the University of Oklahoma than they do with their campus faculty colleagues in education. Disciplinary and professional associations offer a means to connect with far-flung colleagues with common interests. Indeed, these connections may more accurately be reconnections, as graduate school friends meet "same time, next year" with colleagues now distributed across the region, country, or globe.

Service to Students

In addition to their service to the institution and their disciplines, faculty members also serve their students in areas that reach far beyond the obvious service of teaching. Service to students might include advising, counseling, and letters of recommendation. In addition, faculty in most graduate programs and some undergraduate programs work with students on research through proposal and thesis writing. Advising is one aspect of service to students, but advising is often much more extensive than helping a student pick a few courses out of a catalogue and stamping a schedule sheet (Lords, 2000). A scholar who takes advising responsibilities seriously soon finds herself offering career and personal counseling.

Graduate students also require advising (and often counseling) as well as additional assistance with proposals and dissertations. Helping one student generate a proposal and see it through to a defense can be a time-consuming (albeit rewarding) experience. Assisting fifteen or twenty students simultaneously can quickly become overwhelming, particularly at the end of a semester, when finals, grades, and proposal and dissertation defenses often pile up in a professor's date book.

Advising is a role that transcends both teaching and service. It can be viewed as part of out-of-classroom teaching responsibilities (as when meeting with a student in office hours and ending up giving career advising), but it is also part of service responsibilities in that it is typically not paid and only ambiguously rewarded. Furthermore, in liberal arts colleges and other residential settings, there tend to be more connections between faculty and students, with faculty commonly called on to advise student groups, direct undergraduate research programs, and contribute more fully to the campus (Prince, 2000). In this way, service can be viewed as an extension of teaching, which on the liberal arts campus is the primary focus. This leads to an interesting question about the advising: Is it part of the teaching role, or is it part of the service role? For purposes of this monograph, advising that is done one to one with students as part of a class or curriculum is considered teaching. Advising of groups of students (for example, the Spanish Club) falls under the rubric of internal service, even though this type of service certainly has a teaching component. Advising graduate student research bridges all three roles, since it encompasses teaching, research, and service.

Advising is understood to take up part of the faculty member's time, but that portion of time is often thought of as fixed, when in fact it can grow. In a cruel twist, a professor who gains a reputation as a successful or popular adviser or chair is approached by more and more students for assistance. The advising load grows, but the time allotted to a scholar to complete her work remains constant.

Advising, and service to students in general, is understood to be part of the faculty member's job, but the product of advising does not always appear on a vita or a tenure review file. Service to students is valued (given lip-service) but rarely rewarded, and time spent in advising keeps the scholar from the work that is rewarded (Boice, 2000). This is the crux of the tension so many faculty face in their work lives. Students see their concerns as immediate and do not recognize that the ten minutes they request (which often stretches to thirty minutes or more) can set a research project or class preparation back. Faculty who attempt to draw boundaries, however, find themselves criticized by both students and administration as being unavailable or unconcerned.

> **Service to students is valued but rarely rewarded, and time spent in advising keeps the scholar from the work that is rewarded. This is the crux of the tension so many faculty face in their work lives.**

Indeed, it is this aspect of expected but unrewarded service (to students, but also to the institution) that fills the day of the faculty member and leads to people working on research on weekends or late at night. Office hours are filled with student and departmental concerns, forcing research and class preparation into the time that is left. Here lies part of the dilemma of a committed faculty member: from the standpoint of collegiality, departmental meetings and student concerns are primary, followed by class preparation and teaching, with research productivity a distant third. Yet when faculty rewards are evaluated, research is most important, teaching an acknowledged second, and service an expected but unremarkable third component (Berberet, 2002; Tierney and Bensimon, 1996).

The Difference That Difference Makes

The limited literature that focuses on faculty service roles tends to look at faculty homogeneously. Faculty work, however, is shaped by many factors: discipline, the size of the institution, promotion and tenure standards, workplace norms and cultures, personal experience, gender, race, and other background and institutional characteristics.

With few exceptions (Antonio and others, 2000; O'Meara, 2002), faculty service literature has not paid much attention to the influence of factors such as race and ethnicity, institutional type, gender, and rank on an individual's involvement in service (and, for the purposes of this chapter, to internal service specifically). Some of the literature, however, does suggest that faculty work is not approached or distributed uniformly (Alger, 2000; Baez, 2000; Bensimon and others, 2000; Clark, 1987, Eason, 1996; Tierney and Bensimon, 1996; Garcia, 2000; Turner, 2002; Turner and Myers, 2000). While it is fair to say that service is overlooked and ambiguously defined yet ubiquitous for all faculty, special attention must be given to some of the dimensions of difference to see what impact they have on faculty and the service roles they undertake. Here I review the topics of institutional type, discipline, rank and experience, and the demographic variables of gender and race to shed light on how these categories influence internal service roles.

Institutional Type

Faculty involvement in decision making varies by institutional type. "As one moves up the status hierarchy, one encounters more professional control, and as one moves down, one observes more administrative dominance and even autocracy" (Clark, 1987, p. 161). At research universities, faculties maintain control over areas of university policy that affect their work directly, such as human subjects review. For faculty at larger and more prestigious campuses (and especially faculty who are tenured), this means that they have greater personal power and professional autonomy, which typically translates to fewer service obligations tied to the institution (Austin and Gamson, 1983). Service for faculty at these institutions tends to be focused outward on national activity and reputation, as well as funding agencies. As one moves further down the institutional scale, administration begins to take precedence in the setting of policy for faculty, who are treated more as employees contracted to teach than as equals in the governing of the campus (Austin and Gamson, 1983).

Faculty members in community colleges tend to encounter managerial cultures—that is, systems with more administrative oversight than faculty governance. This occurs because many community colleges evolved out of a secondary school system that relied heavily on local and administrative control (Clark, 1987). Furthermore, on today's community college campuses, adjuncts often outnumber full-time faculty, leaving a limited cadre of faculty to engage in campus service. On community college campuses, this has come to mean either an overworked full-time faculty taking on increased service responsibilities or increasing emphasis on managerial decision making. In short,

> *At the top of the institutional hierarchy faculty influence is well and strong. Many individuals have strong personal bargaining power; departments and professional schools are strong, semi-autonomous units; and all-campus faculty bodies have dominant influence in personnel and curricular decisions. University presidents speak lovingly of the faculty as the core of the institution and walk gently around entrenched faculty prerogatives. As we descend the hierarchy, however, faculty authority weakens and managerialism increases* [Clark, 1987, p. 170].

There are mitigating factors in this rather broad classification. The small size of some liberal arts institutions can help to create cohesiveness among the faculty that is not readily available at a large research university (Prince, 2000). In some of the larger research universities, a faculty member may only know colleagues in her unit or lab; indeed, some departments are so large that many members are strangers to each other (to say nothing of the fact that often few professors are conversant with the research of their colleagues). Furthermore, faculty members at smaller liberal arts schools are often required to teach a broader spectrum of courses than do their counterparts at research universities. This means they are more likely to overlap expertise with other faculty. In addition, at liberal arts colleges, there tend to be more connections between faculty and students, with faculty commonly called on to advise student groups, direct undergraduate research programs, and contribute more fully to the campus. As flatter organizations with fewer faculty members, liberal arts college faculty tend to have more involvement in service.

Most campuses use processes of shared governance, but how the input of faculty is received and used is variable. Institutional culture and leadership styles also weigh heavily in how much involvement faculty have in governance. Leaders seeking to maintain the collegium and who operate as a first among equals tend to invite faculty input on major decisions, whereas leaders looking to maintain control and coordination tend to rely on bureaucratic structures for compliance (Bensimon, Neumann, and Birnbaum, 1989). Faculty involvement in institutional affairs can vary considerably based on leadership and institutional culture, in addition to discipline and type of institution (Fairweather, 1996; Leslie, 2002).

Institutional type can influence both the type and the degree of involvement of a faculty member's campus-based internal service. As a broad classification, professors at research institutions have more autonomy and control over aspects of their departments than do faculty at other types of campuses. They have more to say in admissions and curricular decisions than do their counterparts at institutions with more managerial cultures. Faculty at these research institutions may have extensive service commitments to their departments or colleges, but their input counts. At community colleges, which tend to be more managerial, professors still have extensive service obligations to their institutions, but their involvement has less impact on final decision making (Miller, Vacik, and Benton, 1998).

Discipline

Although there is only limited research about disciplinary norms and how they shape faculty work, and in particular faculty at work as institutional and disciplinary citizens, they undoubtedly do. In general, disciplinary and professional associations do not dictate standards for faculty work (Diamond and Adam, 1995; Leslie, 2002), and those associations that do tend to be more general in these standards (for example, on teaching, research, service, and scholarship). Variability in opportunities for funding, accreditation, and types of research can distance disciplines and departments from one another and shape how they view faculty work (Leslie, 2002). When considering aspects of faculty work such as service, typically disciplines on different campuses are more alike than are different disciplines on the same campus. For example, education faculty, regardless of campus, can expect service responsibilities with local schools (Brown, 1994; Hill and Pope, 1995; Lawson, 1996).

Disciplinary affiliation does have an impact on faculty internal service because disciplines rely heavily on faculty to maintain the activities of disciplinary associations:

> *Organized around individual subjects, the disciplines have their own histories and trajectories, their own habits and practices. Going concerns in their own right, they also couple their members to national and international groups of scholars and researchers. As they promote affiliations that slash across institutions, they turn "locals" into "cosmopolitans"* [Clark, 1987, p. 25].

These "cosmopolitan" faculty are those who are more tied to their disciplinary peers than to institutional colleagues, whereas the "locals" tend to be more focused on the institution and campus colleagues. Disciplinary activity ranging from attending conferences to leading disciplinary organizations adds dimensions to the service part of the equation of faculty work. First, cosmopolitan faculty tend to be more involved with their disciplines in terms of service because they are maintaining the functioning of the organization and, to that end, the internal functioning of the discipline. Second, disciplinary activity and involvement can shift local orientations into cosmopolitan outlooks. "Professors are never the same after they have tasted the delights of subject specialties that join them to far-flung peers" (Clark, 1987, p. 25). From the standpoint of internal institutional functioning, too many faculty members with a cosmopolitan focus can mean a lack of local faculty to do the work of supporting the institution through shared governance (Berberet, 2002; Burgan, 1998).

This "duality of enterprise and discipline is inherent in modern higher education" (Clark, 1987, p. 26), and it is perhaps this duality that is at the crux of the challenges between campus and community concerns. The campus is organized by discipline, which is not always an appropriate organizing schema for working with communities (Zlotkowski, 2000, 2001). Perhaps contemporary challenges regarding service are tied to higher education's not being neatly organized in ways that allow for the fulfillment of the outreach and public service component of faculty work. (I will expand further on this notion when I address connections between the different service roles of faculty and how these come together to promote the better internal and external functions of higher education.)

Rank and Experience

Faculty time and involvement with internal service varies by rank and experience as well. Research on faculty shows that participation in and influence on institutional affairs is dictated, in part, by an individual's rank (Austin and Gamson, 1983; Finkelstein, 1984). Knowledge about institutional and disciplinary affairs grows as one gains more experience as a professor in general and as a professor at one campus in particular.

At the institutional level, tenure and rank are required to serve in some influential service positions (for example, promotion and tenure committees). At the disciplinary level, rank and experience typically confer visibility and experience, which are often both prerequisite for service positions of higher prestige and power in organizations. Austin and Gamson (1983), using earlier research by Baldwin and Blackburn (1981), found in their work on the academic workplace that "the third component of faculty work, service, appears to increase over the years. Faculty members appear to get more involved in service activities as they become more comfortable with their teaching responsibilities and less pressured by demands for scholarship" (p. 22).

New faculty members face many challenges as they begin a new profession with relatively little preparation. Academic communities have tacitly assumed that content knowledge in a particular area prepares one for the intricacies of faculty life (Boice, 1995, 2000). A graduate program may well prepare a student in the details of research, and many (although not all) new professors will have taught or taken teaching courses in graduate school. Those who are fortunate enough to have good mentoring as graduate students and then good direction as new faculty members may find the transition from graduate school to a faculty position to be manageable and the transition from writing a dissertation to directing one seamless. New faculty who have not had effective mentoring in the navigation of faculty life and the tenure track, whether that mentoring occurred in graduate school or at the new institution, face an uphill battle as they seek to balance the demands of teaching, research, and service.

In particular, the new faculty member may face service overload. Service represents an immediate connection with others in the campus or disciplinary community, and a moderate involvement in service responsibilities is a good way to integrate oneself into an institution and the profession (Boice, 1992, 2000). In addition, service commitments can seem easy, at least in comparison to some of the more daunting tasks associated with teaching and research. Although some campuses give new faculty a service honeymoon (a year without extensive service requirements) to adjust to the demands of establishing syllabi, teaching courses, and beginning research, soon enough the new colleague will find himself serving on department and university committees and assisting on student committees. In hopes of establishing a rapport with campus colleagues, a faculty member can easily find herself volunteering (and being volunteered into) many hours of service, often to the detriment of teaching and research. Faculty from groups traditionally outside the academic mainstream can find the balancing act particularly tricky.

Race and Gender

Increasingly, both anecdotal and research-based evidence supports the notion that people who are different from historical norms in the professoriat are called on disproportionately to serve their units, campuses, disciplinary associations, and communities (Aguirre, 2000). For a faculty member whose gender or ethnicity is unusual on a campus or in a department, this difference can translate into frequent calls to represent their gender or ethnicity in organizational and disciplinary affairs. Padilla (1994) refers to this as *cultural taxation* and Kolodny (1998) as *hidden workload*.

This cultural taxation often occurs in service-related activities: a biologist serving on the Women in the Sciences task force, a lesbian asked to advise a student program for lesbians, an African American professor representing minority faculty on a number of search committees. These activities tend to be less valued by promotion and tenure committees than are teaching and research, and the ethnic or gender or sexual orientation component can exacerbate this devaluation, as institutions also tend to devalue work supporting causes affiliated with race and gender (Aguirre, 2000; Alger, 2000; Garcia, 2000; Tierney and Bensimon, 1996; Padilla, 1994; Turner and Myers, 2000). Negotiating this dilemma can create challenging tensions for minority faculty, particularly junior faculty. On the one hand, the new minority scholar faces a desire or an obligation to represent an interest group, either because no one else is available or because the individual is interested in having a viewpoint represented (Baez, 2000). On the other hand, excessive participation in undervalued service activities can lead to falling behind in the more highly valued areas of research and teaching (Alger, 2000; Tierney and Bensimon, 1996; Padilla, 1994).

Scholars who are members of more than one underrepresented group can find this dilemma doubly troubling. They may be asked to represent several constituencies in a variety of activities, further reducing their time and opportunity to focus on research and teaching. Turner and Myers (2000) have called the multiple marginalization of women of color on the basis of gender and race a "double whammy."

Race- and gender-based service presents a double bind for the new faculty member in particular, as Padilla (1994) aptly described:

> *First, as students and then as professionals, we are often told that although diversity may be important, it is not a substitute for intellectual excellence and that we must develop more than ethnic competencies in our training. In fact, our competencies must be in a substantive content area, plus research methodology, and, of course,*

we must publish. However, at the first sign of trouble with an ethnic student or client, the administration relinquishes responsibility and calls upon a resident ethnic faculty member or graduate student(s) to deal with diversity experiences that the administration is unable to manage on its own. Unfortunately, the eventual "payback" for such service is, in the case of the student, the warning that too much time is being spent on ethnic matters and too little on one's graduate program, or in the case of the junior professional, threat of loss of job security and advancement within the organization. Many nonethnic administrators fail to understand that ethnic issues cannot be turned on and off like a faucet, and that the crisis may be far from resolved even though the administration may no longer hear about the program. In fact, the ethnic person may be spending considerable time working behind the scenes to keep things calm [p. 26].

On predominantly white campuses, where there tend to be few minority faculty, the issue of tokenism is acute. As tokens, faculty are asked to represent their category (race, gender, sexual orientation) on committees as a way to help campuses accomplish goals for diversity (Aguirre, 2000; Baez, 2000). In this way, minority members of the faculty find themselves overworked in fulfilling campus missions for diversity.

The hidden workload that minority faculty members face is an often-cited reason that professors from outside the traditional white male bastion of academe have difficulty meeting the academic standards set for tenure. The problem is not that these scholars are incapable of generating successful scholarship; the problem is that they can easily find themselves tied up in the service dilemma that faces all junior faculty, plus the burden of the hidden workload of service based on their race, gender, or other identifying trait.

Service expectations based on race and gender exist not only for internal service. Service to the community and public service may also present expectations that a scholar will meet the needs of communities outside the university in specific ways, the subject of the following chapter.

Conclusion

An essential step in creating and fostering an engaged campus and an involved faculty will be finding appropriate ways to recognize and reward service to the university, the department, the discipline, and students, that is, internal service. Until reward structures reflect the importance of these service activities to the work of an engaged faculty, scholars will feel trapped in a service bind: service, especially within the university but also without, is expected of faculty members, but that service is rarely rewarded during promotion and tenure reviews. Instead, service commitments are often seen as having kept a scholar from establishing or furthering a research agenda, publishing, securing grants, or maintaining high standards of teaching.

> **An essential step in creating and fostering an engaged campus and an involved faculty will be finding appropriate ways to recognize and reward service to the university, the department, the discipline, and students, that is, internal service.**

On the one hand, faculty members are told that service is an important and necessary part of their jobs, but on the other, they are told not to let service commitments keep them from the more "important" roles of teaching and, especially, research. Until faculty reward structures change to recognize service, faculty will continue to view their service commitments as necessary evils or impediments to their professional progress. With this outlook, service is not viewed as a part of one's job as scholar; instead, service is viewed as something that has to be taken care of before a scholar can begin the real work of a professor. These attitudes are detrimental to the values of the profession (Burgan, 1998).

Faculty involvement with the institutional community through internal service encourages the effective functioning of higher education institutions. If campuses want to be primed for engagement with external communities and to realize campus goals for outreach, they must be prepared internally. Campuses rely on a healthy relationship between faculty institutional service and institutional vitality to function effectively: "A service compact between faculty and their institutions is critically needed—both for the well-being of the faculty community and institutional health and to enhance higher education's contribution to society" (Berberet, 1999, p. 34).

External Service: Faculty at Work Meeting Societal Needs

THE TEACHING, RESEARCH, AND SERVICE trivium is the standard by which faculty are rewarded at most colleges and universities. Service, although typically less clearly defined than the other two aspects of faculty work, is included in a majority of promotion and tenure guidelines and faculty job descriptions. For faculty, service means supporting their institutions through involvement in institutional governance roles (internal service) and by translating institutional missions of public service and outreach to the public by making teaching and research relevant and connected to community and societal needs. Outreach is a mission-related concept that connects the resources of higher education with audiences external to campus (Lynton, 1995). One of the ways this function is fulfilled is through the service roles of faculty. A historical look at the service mission of higher education points to a long tradition of faculty outreach and service (Finkelstein, 1984; O'Meara, 1997; Bringle and others, 1999; Ehrlich, 1995).

Outreach is a mission-related concept that connects the resources of higher education with audiences external to campus.

In the light of current conversations about the scholarship of engagement and renewed interest in the engaged campus, service to external communities (defined here as external service but also called outreach) has been given renewed attention by faculty, administrators, researchers, and other stakeholders of higher education. External service roles of faculty are a way for higher education to communicate clearly to its multiple publics what faculty do in the realms of teaching, research, and service. As a fundamental component of higher education, Fear and Sandmann (1995) identify outreach as a "form of scholarship that cuts across teaching, research, and service" (p. 113). Furthermore, based on definitions generated from Michigan State University, Fear and Sandmann explain outreach as "generating, transmitting, applying, and preserving knowledge for the direct benefit of external audiences that are consistent with university and unit missions" (p. 113).

There are different ways that faculty meet the needs of the external audiences of higher education. This chapter explores the external service roles of faculty by examining the work they do that is associated with extension, consulting, service-learning, and community and civic service. It is these aspects of faculty work that support and meet community needs.

A Word About Nomenclature

In recent years, the external service work of faculty and of institutions in general has been called many things and defined in many different ways. Lynton (1995), in his important work, defines professional service as "work by faculty members based on their scholarly expertise and contributing to the mission of the institution" (p. 1). In this definition, he subsumes the term *outreach* as well, since he ties professional service to the outreach mission of a campus: "Through outreach a university or a college becomes a direct intellectual resource for its external constituencies" (p. 1). By enacting professional service roles, faculty realize institutional outreach missions.

Fear and Sandmann (1995) note that "making knowledge accessible for the direct benefit of persons and entities external to the academy (i.e., outreach) is a vital part of what a university is supposed to do. When a university *extends itself* to meet the knowledge needs of persons, groups, and institutions, university outreach takes place" (p. 112). Fear and Sandmann (1995) focus on higher education as a knowledge enterprise and see outreach roles supporting knowledge generation, discovery, and application (Lynton and Elman, 1987; Thomas, 1998; Sandmann and others, 2000; Ramaley, 2000).

Based on their experience at Michigan State University and the redefinition of university outreach on that campus, Fear and Sandmann (1995) define university outreach as "a form of scholarship that cuts across teaching, research, and service. It involves generating, transmitting, applying, and preserving knowledge for the direct benefit of external audiences in ways that are consistent with university and unit missions" (p. 113). At Michigan State University, outreach is a "mission-related activity of the university, . . . rooted in scholarship" (p. 113). This chapter highlights how faculty service roles and institutional outreach missions support connections between the knowledge enterprise and societal needs beyond the campus.

When discussing external service, it is important to distinguish the work that faculty perform that extends beyond the campus to address community needs and that applies disciplinary expertise (Sandmann and others, 2000). Not all service roles apply or require an individual's scholarly expertise, and not all are deemed scholarship. In an attempt to clarify and delineate the external service roles of faculty, following is a description of the ways faculty enact these roles.

Extension

The foundation of the land grant college movement was to put higher education in direct service to the public (Campbell, 1998). Originally enacted to support the connection between land grant colleges and agricultural communities, the Smith-Lever Act of 1914 provided funding to place cooperative extension agents, who were also land grant college faculty, in every county in the United States. These agents were key to transferring technology and knowledge from the university community to the community at large. Cooperative extension was created as a conduit to connect land grant campuses with their state communities to fulfill outreach and service missions. Historically, the focus was on the transfer of information to meet agricultural needs. Extension agents were "field representatives" of the university (Rosentreter, 1957, p. 29). Today, extension agents are still in place throughout the country, with expanded roles and service that reach beyond the agricultural arena. These agents are ideally situated to support a variety of campus outreach initiatives. In general, extension agents as faculty in the field provide a link between the expertise of the campus and the needs of the community. Extension provides a local resource with statewide connections to meet the needs of communities in areas ranging from agricultural concerns to economic development to youth programs (Parker, Greenbaum, and Pister, 2001).

The extension infrastructure supports the outreach mission of the campus. In addition to extension agents, other faculty on land grant campuses support community work. A faculty member in animal science who specializes in sheep may simultaneously work on campus doing traditional faculty work and also provide expertise to different communities throughout the state. These professors are not technically extension faculty, but their work can support the mission of extension.

Here is an example of how extension functions today. In Anaconda, Montana, extension agent Barb Andreozzi is a field faculty member of Montana State University and is taking on roles that extend far beyond agriculture and home economics. In her work as a cooperative extension agent for the county, she sees herself as a community redeveloper and a change agent. When a smelter that was the focus of economic activity and the main employer in the town shut down in 1980, the town's population and tax base plummeted. Andreozzi led an economic redevelopment effort to help reenvision the future of Anaconda. She did some of this work herself as an extension agent, but equally important were her efforts to tap into the resources of Montana State University and the University of Montana. Business faculty led workshops on small business development, a graduate student in electrical engineering helped rewire antique lighting downtown, and professors of landscape architecture and building architecture developed plans to update downtown facades. This example illustrates how the role of contemporary cooperative extension agents has changed and how these agents can serve as a conduit to faculty resources on campus (B. Andreozzi, personal communication, 2002; Williams, 1996).

Contemporary extension includes not only activities associated with traditional cooperative extension but also activities of the "extended university" (Lynton and Elman, 1987, p. 148). The traditional extension system, because it is already established within the university system infrastructure, is one readily available bridging mechanism for connecting campuses with their communities. Extending the outreach function of higher education has meant, for some campuses, adding offices for outreach or extension. On some land grant campuses, this has meant shifting the role of cooperative extension.

At Oklahoma State University, the traditional extension function goes far beyond the College of Agriculture and administratively has shifted out of agriculture. Each college-level unit throughout the university has an extension office that operates under the dean for university extension, international, and economic development. Extension offices in each college are charged with extending the university beyond traditional boundaries. Their work includes some of the functions associated with continuing education, including workforce development through noncredit programs (for example, computer training for the U.S. Coast Guard), degree and certificate programs (for example, graduate degree programs in off-site local, regional, and international locations), and developing relationships with off-site organizations to bring faculty and student resources to multiple communities. In addition, college extension offices support applied research and technical assistance needs, publications, community development, and cultural enrichment.

Land grant universities support traditional cooperative extension, with offices in every county throughout the country, where cooperative extension agents are field faculty supporting local ties to agriculture, home economics, and youth development through 4-H programs. Agents are faculty themselves and also are a conduit to faculty resources on campus. This function is limited to land grant universities. Some aspects of the extension model, however, such as extending university services beyond the boundaries of the campus, are present on most campuses. On campuses without an extension unit, continuing education is often the unit that fulfills community needs for workforce development, degree programs, and technical assistance. Continuing education plays a major role in facilitating extension missions.

Land grant universities have typically been associated with rural communities. This association is slowly shifting, as communities housing land grant institutions become more urban and suburban. As a result, cooperative extension agents do more of their work in urban and suburban areas, shifting their focus from agriculture to community development and youth issues.

In higher education today, there is an increased focus on urban institutions and their relationships with communities (Braskamp and Wergin, 1998; Mayfield, Hellwig, and Banks, 1999). For example, the Coalition of Urban and Metropolitan Universities (which includes land grant and other institutions) is dedicated to fulfilling urban grant missions of member campuses by focusing on local urban needs. The concept of service has historic ties and contemporary meaning in both rural and urban settings.

Consulting

Consulting is another aspect of the external service role of faculty members:

> *Faculty consulting can be defined as the application of one's professional and scholarly expertise in the community outside the academic institution.* *Viewed as the natural extension of one's teaching and research activities, both the service function and consulting activities long have been recognized as legitimate expressions of the traditional faculty role and mission of most academic institutions in the United States* [Boyer and Lewis, 1985, p. iv].

Consulting is one of the ways that universities and professors engage with external communities (Lawson, 1996; Rolls, 1998). This extension of faculty expertise offers a variety of benefits to faculty members, universities, and communities:

> *Faculty consultation is a highly desirable way of bringing the intellectual resources of a university to bear on the knowledge needs of external constituencies. . . . In addition to monetary remuneration consulting affords faculty opportunities to keep up-to-date in their fields. It also enhances their ability to relate theory to practice, to incorporate appropriate material into their classes, and to improve their recognition of the relationship of their own specialty to cognate fields* [Lynton and Elman, 1987, p. 42].

While consulting has long been recognized as a legitimate faculty role (Boyer and Lewis, 1985), its place in the overall context of faculty work remains unclear (Rolls, 1998; Von Glinow, 1996). Consulting is typically not explicitly expressed or required in faculty guidelines and therefore is difficult to evaluate and reward (Boyer and Lewis, 1985). Furthermore, many, if not most, consultants are paid for their expertise, which contributes to clouding the issue of the relationship of consulting to other faculty roles (Weissman, 1988). Boyer and Lewis (1985) point out that faculty consulting "is not necessarily limited to income-generating activities" (p. 4), but in many instances, faculty are paid for consulting in their area of expertise. It is the issue of payment that has made consulting a gray area for higher education. If a scholar lends her expertise to an endeavor, is the consulting part of her faculty work, or is it her work as an individual? Should a faculty member be paid for consulting work? If consulting is paid, should it be considered service? Should the payment go to the university? Or is all consulting by definition individual work, performed outside one's faculty role?

One way to clear the discussion is to focus not on pay but on scholarship. A faculty member who is applying disciplinary expertise beyond the campus to external audiences is fulfilling an important professional service, regardless of whether the activity is paid or unpaid (Lynton and Elman, 1987). The faculty member is bringing visibility not only to himself as an individual but also to his institution (Brawer, 1998; Dietrich, 1993). Furthermore, consulting activity keeps faculty current in their field and can augment both teaching and research roles (Mirvis, 1996):

A faculty member who is applying disciplinary expertise beyond the campus to external audiences is fulfilling an important professional service.

> Just as graduate level instruction—especially that occurring in seminars or problem courses and in working individually with graduate students on their research projects—is considered neither pure teaching nor pure research but has the quality of a joint product about it, so too faculty consulting has a similar quality whenever it both extends and reinforces the teaching or research expertise of the individual faculty member [Boyer and Lewis, 1985, p. 4].

Ambiguity about whether consulting is paid and uncertainty about its proper place in faculty roles can overshadow the importance of consulting as a means to fulfill higher education's service and outreach functions (Howsam, 1985). When viewed as an augmentation of existing faculty roles and not as a job unto itself, consulting is a legitimate part of faculty work (Bell and Jones, 1992). The University of Illinois at Urbana-Champaign addresses this issue in *A Faculty Guide for Relating Public Service to the Promotion and Tenure Review Process* (Farmer and Schomberg, 1993). This document acknowledges the important role that consulting can fill in helping the institution meet its outreach mission. The report also acknowledges that not all consulting has the extension of knowledge as its primary goal: "At the same time activities that are engaged in mainly to make money such as running a business of a consulting firm on the side are not part of university public service activities" (cited in Lynton, 1995, p. 93). Consulting as a means to fulfill campus outreach missions is a part of faculty work, whereas consulting as a business that supports faculty economic means is a second job (Braskamp and Wergin, 1998).

Consider, for example, the consulting work of a geology professor who specializes in seismic activity. He is hired by a community to determine if the community is prepared in the event of an earthquake. This faculty member, whether paid or unpaid, is providing important service to the community and is also extending disciplinary expertise to audiences beyond the campus. In contrast, if this same faculty member was developing a product (say, community earthquake kits) and then selling them nationwide in addition to giving workshops, this would be considered beyond the faculty role and more of a business. Such work shifts from service into independent work that is primarily fulfilling individual needs as opposed to institutional ones. Granted, the distinction can be difficult to draw. Even when the faculty member stands to benefit privately from consulting activity, he may also be providing public benefits based on disciplinary expertise (Friedman, 1993).

Consulting provides opportunities and limitations (Philips, Regan, Medvene, and Oslin, 1993). For faculty who are consulting outside the university yet using their disciplinary expertise (and often the resources of their positions), questions arise: Are they consulting as individuals or as representatives of an institution? Are they doing consulting work on university time? Perhaps the reason there has been so much concern about faculty consulting is that it can be impossible to separate faculty as individuals from faculty as a college or university employee. If a professor uses the office printer to desktop-publish a consulting workbook, the line is somewhat easy to draw. When faculty are working from their homes, the line between personal and professional time can be more difficult to mark. Also, there is no clear delineation between personal and professional expertise. For example, if a management professor teaches human resource management, performs research in the area, and then consults in her specialty, it is nearly impossible to determine what work is professorial and what work is professional (paid consulting). Additional research is necessary to determine the opportunity costs for consulting and whether consulting time comes out of university time or individual and leisure time (Boyer and Lewis, 1985; Friedman, 1993; Howsam, 1985). Furthermore, additional research is required about the connection between consulting and how it relates to the realization of campus and faculty missions for outreach and service, not to mention the murky issue of consulting with political organizations, religious organizations, or otherwise controversial groups. Additional discussion must also ensue about limits to faculty autonomy with regard to consulting and at what point an institution can ask a faculty member not to participate in certain types of consulting activities.

One area of external service and an extension of consulting that is often overlooked is faculty involvement in governmental affairs. The Wisconsin idea specifically called on faculty members to lend their expertise to the government. In today's colleges and university settings this important outreach role is often overlooked and underutilized (Hy, Venhaus, and Sims, 1995). At a time when higher education often finds itself under fire from governmental entities and other constituencies, knowledge exchange can create positive connections (Walshok, 1995). Faculty have an important role to play in economic development and legislative decision-making that can extend from these connections (Hy, Venhaus, and Sims, 1995; Udell, 1990). University think tanks and research centers are also part of this information exchange and need to more fully exercise and claim their public service role (Melnick, 1999).

Service-Learning

The integration of community service into academic course work is another way for faculty to enact campus outreach missions. Service-learning has been defined by Rhoads and Howard (1998) as a "pedagogical model that intentionally integrates academic learning and relevant community service" (p. 1). Jacoby (1996) adds to this with her definition:

> *Service-learning is a form of experiential education in which students engage in activities that address human and community needs together with structured opportunities intentionally designed to promote student learning and development. Reflection and reciprocity are key concepts of service-learning* [p. 5].

Service-learning provides a means for faculty, students, and the university to engage with the community. Furthermore, well-designed service-learning opportunities provide a way for faculty to integrate and unify teaching, research, and service roles (Cushman, 1999; Mettetal and Bryant, 1996).

The work of Marian McKenna, a professor of literacy studies at the University of Montana, illustrates the overlap of roles. Through a service-learning component in her courses, she places students in area community agencies, including the adult basic education center and a refugee assistance program. The service efforts of her students have helped her establish relationships with the community through the partnerships that have developed through service-learning. These partnerships in turn have created opportunities for research collaboration. In addition, expertise about service-learning and partnership development has yielded opportunity for disciplinary service and consulting. As a faculty member, McKenna is enacting her external service roles in multiple ways—through teaching using service-learning, through research on service-learning and literacy strategies, and through consulting—as she has shared her expertise through in-service programs and also through other opportunities resulting from connections established through service-learning courses. In addition, she has enacted internal service roles through participation on campus, state, and disciplinary committees related to service-learning. McKenna's work illustrates the way traditional academic boundaries blur when faculty apply their expertise to meet community needs (Lynton, 1998; Magrath, 1999; Votruba, 1996).

Service-learning is an integrated strategy because faculty are simultaneously enacting service roles and teaching roles (and, potentially, research roles, as indicated in the example above). Service-learning brings community into the classroom (Jay, 2000; Maloney, 2000). In terms of institutional priorities and faculty rewards, service-learning needs to be defined and linked to institutional mission (Hirsh and Lynton, 1995). "If tenure is linked to institutional priorities, a faculty member skilled in an area of service linked to an institutional priority is more likely to be awarded tenure" (O'Meara, 1997, p. 5). That is, if campuses value teaching and outreach, service-learning is a way for faculty to help realize campus missions. Service-learning, like other forms of outreach, succeeds best when faculty are rewarded for their efforts to reach out and engage the community (Ward, 1998).

> **Service-learning is an end unto itself in terms of a pedagogical strategy, but it is also a way to reenvision relationships between campus and community, student and content, faculty and student.**

Service-learning is an end unto itself in terms of a pedagogical strategy, but it is also a way to reenvision relationships between campus and community, student and content, faculty and student (Arches and others, 1997; Sannders, 1998; Wagner, 1987; Zlotkowski, 1997). The spheres of faculty work are typically viewed separately, but service-learning provides a framework of unity (Cushman, 1999). "In many ways, service-learning cuts across all three areas and includes faculty work in teaching, research, and service" (Kezar and Rhoads, 2001, p. 158). The challenge lies in encouraging campuses to acknowledge this view of service-learning and reward it accordingly. In addition, there is a need for ongoing assessment of service-learning and its effectiveness for engaging students in service and learning (Eyler and Giles, 1999; Gray, Ondaatje, Fricker, and Geschwind, 2000; Hesser, 1995; Kezar, 2002; Sax and Astin, 1997).

Cushman (1999) offers an integrated view for how service-learning can provide unity for faculty work. In this framework, teaching, research, and service done in a community-based tradition contribute to each sector of faculty work simultaneously.

The research contributes

- To teaching by informing a curriculum that responds to both students' and community members' needs, and
- To service by indicating emerging problems in the community which the students and curriculum address.

The teaching contributes

- To research by generating fieldnotes, papers, taped interactions, and other materials, and
- To service by facilitating the community organization's programmatic goals with the volunteer work.

The service contributes

- To research by addressing political and social issues salient in everyday life struggles, and
- To teaching by offering students and professors avenues for testing the utility of previous scholarship in light of community members' daily lives and cultural values [Cushman, 1999, p. 331].

Cushman's conceptualization illustrates the synergy that can exist between different faculty roles and how service-learning (and other external service roles as well) facilitates the process. This synergy captures the work of the engaged campus. Although many colleges and universities are still challenged with envisioning how to integrate the tripartite nature of faculty work (Votruba, 1996), faculty experiences with service-learning have established steps in this direction.

On many campuses, increased faculty involvement in service-learning has led to questions about faculty rewards (Stanton, 1990; Ward, 1998).

Specifically, are faculty rewarded for service-learning? Where does service-learning fit in terms of teaching, research, and service? Is it service? Is it teaching? Boyer's work (1990) to broaden definitions of scholarship has been instrumental in leading campuses to rethink the possibilities of new definitions of scholarship and of integrated views of scholarship. Notable examples include Portland State University and California State University-Monterey Bay. Both campuses use Boyer's framework for scholarship in their promotion and tenure documents. Faculty are rewarded for contributions they make to discovery, integration, application, and teaching in place of traditional teaching, research, and service. The Boyer model helps these campuses more directly meet their regional missions for community engagement and local problem solving. When scholars are acknowledged and rewarded for their efforts to embrace and extend the scholarship of engagement, they are finding their efforts to be both personally gratifying and professionally rewarded (Driscoll, Sandmann, and Foster-Fishman, 2000; Gelmon and Agre-Kippenhan, 2002; Williams, 2000).

Community-Based Action Research

Clearly blurring boundaries between research and external service (and even teaching if students are involved) is community-based action research. This approach to research engages researchers, students, and community leaders "in a collaborative process of critical inquiry into problems of social practice in a learning context" (cited in Couto, 2001, p. 4). Action-based research holds an important place in conversations about external service because it has the potential to make public the disciplinary work of the academy. It also has the potential to encourage interdisciplinary work, as most community problems do not come in disciplinary packages. Community problems typically require a complex analytical approach that involves expertise in several different disciplines and methodological genres (Votruba, 1996; Zlotkowski, 2000, 2001).

Community-based action research is distinct from traditional research in process and outcome. As a process, this approach to research involves community members in roles typically taken on by academic researchers—that is, as researchers (Kemmis and McTaggart, 2000). As a collaborative, researchers and community participants investigate problems of mutual concern. Action research is typically presented in multiple venues as a way to communicate findings to both academic and community colleagues. Marian McKenna, the literacy professor engaged in service-learning, provides an example of how community-based action research might work. Through connections with the adult basic education center in her community, McKenna and her community partners may see a need to know more about family reading habits. This inquiry could emerge out of her interest in the literacy strategies of young children and the adult basic education center's interest in supporting adults as readers. Based on common interests, the research project would develop.

Action-based research does for traditional research what service-learning does for traditional teaching.

In addition to typical scholarly venues, McKenna and her community partners could write about their work in the center newsletter and present their findings to the local United Way as part of an effort for funding for literacy projects. In this way, action-based research meets an important goal of communicating the aims of research to external (and varied) audiences. It also is a way for researchers to convey their responsibilities as social researchers (Fine, Weis, Weseen, and Wong, 2000). Action-based research does for traditional research what service-learning does for traditional teaching.

Community and Civic Service

In addition to their work as faculty members, professors engage their communities through the individual work that they do as private citizens. Service performed by faculty for and with the community falls under the category of community and civic service (Ward, 2002). Essentially, this type of service is volunteerism. Typically, faculty contributing civic service do so independent of their roles on campus; they might, for example, collect food for a food drive. If faculty are involved in civic service that is tied to their discipline, as when an accounting professor provides financial advice and direction to a homeless shelter, this service would be considered differently since it is tied to faculty expertise. The accounting example would be a case of unpaid consulting.

Most promotion and tenure guidelines request a listing of community involvements of faculty as citizens. While these involvements are not rewarded as central faculty roles, they are acknowledged as faculty playing a leadership role in their communities. In smaller communities, in particular, faculty members often make valuable contributions as citizens and community members. These roles should be acknowledged. Faculty are representatives of their campus, and the work they do in the community, whether directly tied to faculty roles or not, is a way for the community to see what faculty do. For example, at Mars Hill College, a small, rural campus in western North Carolina, a strong history between campus and community and a regional focus of the campus place faculty in constant contact with the community. Promotion and tenure guidelines around service highlight civic involvement to meet community needs.

Much of the confusion in the discussion of service and its evaluation and reward has been tied in part to confusion about what faculty do as private citizens, what they do as representatives of their campuses, and what they do that is tied to their disciplinary expertise. For example, the faculty member helping to lead a fundraising campaign on campus to support United Way is performing as a representative to the campus, but this work is not specifically tied to the professor's expertise and thus would not be tied to a scholarly agenda. The University of Illinois distinguishes between public service and private service in order to distinguish between service that is atheoretical and distinct from faculty expertise and service that is grounded in discipline. Public service is performed in fulfillment of the mission of the campus and is tied to disciplinary expertise. Private service is defined as the outreach done by faculty as independent citizens (referred to here as community and civic service).

The Difference That Difference Makes

Generally, all faculty members are expected to be involved in the fulfillment of the service mission of their campuses, although the precise nature of their involvement varies greatly from individual to individual and campus to campus. Expectations for faculty to perform service roles, particularly outreach roles, are significantly affected by institutional type, discipline, and rank, as well as demographic characteristics like race and gender. Following is a description of how these differences manifest themselves with regard to the external service roles.

Institutional Type

The range of higher education institutional diversity in the United States rests fundamentally on different visions of what civic responsibility involves and how it should be promoted or instilled in citizens. Central to the mission of land grant universities was service to society through the generation of new knowledge and its application to specific problems. Technical universities, founded at the end of the nineteenth century at a time of great faith in technology and progress, extended that tradition, confident that the well-being of society would be ensured by citizens well trained in science and technology. Since the 1960s, community colleges have defined their mission as being a gateway to helping citizens enter society economically, politically, and socially. The United States has benefited immensely from this diversity and its collective effect on promoting civic responsibility. Conversely, no single form of higher education should claim special privilege in this effort (Prince, 2000).

Faculty service roles and corresponding rewards vary significantly by the mission of the institution, which in turn varies depending on the classification of the institution. Although a majority of campuses make reference to service or its related nomenclature (for example, public service, civic service, outreach, or engagement) in their mission statements, how this service is enacted on campuses is variable. For some campuses, talk of service is mostly rhetoric, and service roles are fulfilled largely through institutional and disciplinary citizenship (faculty involvement in internal service) and general citizenship (faculty involvement with community, civic, and private service) (Gamson, 1997; Lynton, 1995). On other campuses, service roles have been embraced as active concepts for students and faculty to pursue.

As service has become an important higher education topic, institutional type has played a major role in the ways that campuses have sought to enact their service missions. The service movement and discussions of engaged campuses have affected most higher educational institutions, and different categories of campuses have responded to the call for engagement differently. In all sectors of higher education, there have been calls to honor the historical tradition of service, but the tenor of the resurgence varies based on the goals of individual campuses. Much of this variation stems from the classification of the institution (Roberts, Wergin, and Adam, 1993).

Community Colleges. The very name *community college* suggests the importance of community and outreach in the fabric of these institutions. Indeed, this emphasis on community is "the very essence of the community college—what makes it distinctly different from other types of colleges and universities" (Crosson, 1983, p. 28). The outreach function of the community college is fulfilled through diverse educational opportunities for a diverse group of students, lifelong learning, cultural events, and, increasingly, service-learning (Crosson, 1983; Elsner, 2000; Hirose-Wong, 1999; Robinson, 1999). The American Association of Community Colleges has been instrumental in supporting campus initiatives to expand the role of service-learning (Robinson, 1999, 2000). The whole mission of the campus is centered on community needs. Given the lack of prevalence of traditional research on community college campuses, outreach functions are more focused on curriculum, teaching, and other types of endeavors that bring the community into the college and the college into the community (Lee, 1997; Peterman, 2000).

Community colleges by definition are connected to their supporting communities, and these connections encourage outreach and engagement. Many factors affect this connection. Students tend to be from a narrower geographic range than is true for other types of institutions, and curricula tend to be more focused on adult basic educational functions and vocational programs than at other types of campuses. Open admissions policies and community connections encourage community colleges to develop and refine curricula to meet varied and changing community needs (Cohen, 1998; Robinson, 1999, 2000). Many community colleges partner with local industries to meet emergent needs and help develop the local workforce (Carnevale and Desrochers, 2001). Furthermore, community colleges as community development agencies serve as a central point for planning and implementing projects to improve the economic and social viability of the community served (Parsons, 1989).

Comprehensive Colleges and Universities. Comprehensive institutions offer a wide range of baccalaureate degree programs and graduate education through the master's degree. Many of these campuses have a regional focus (they are also called regional universities) and were founded as teachers' colleges or normal schools (Cohen, 1998). Cohen (1998) notes that these campuses resembled community colleges, given their focus on bachelor's and master's degree programs. In addition, they have "a strong affinity for a particular region. Usually, the mission of these institutions carries a special responsibility to the needs of a particular place and a particular population" (Ramaley, 2000b, p. 231).

In the hierarchy of higher education, comprehensive institutions occupy an interesting niche. As regional campuses, they can attempt to be all things to all people—offering programs to meet regional needs at the associate, bachelor's, and graduate levels. For some comprehensives, this has meant a challenge to remaining true to the comprehensive and regional mission, as focus has shifted to drifting upward to become more like traditional research universities (Aldersley, 1995; Boyer, 1990; Finnegan, 1993; Ramaley, 2000b). This has been particularly true in the light of scarce resources. Research activity, that is, grant acquisition and faculty entrepreneurship, can aid campuses by bringing in external funds, but these activities tend to move faculty focus beyond immediate campus and community needs (Clark, 1983; Finnegan, 1993). In this way, the quest for prestige can beguile campuses with the "promise of prestige associated with doctoral level education" (Aldersley, 1995, p. 56).

Regional and comprehensive universities have an opportunity, however, to grow and modernize while moving beyond mimicry of traditional research universities. They may be able to realize their missions, focusing on community and regional needs, while embracing innovative ways of combining their teaching, research, and service missions (Rice, 1996b; Ramaley, 2000b). Portland State University serves as a prime example of a regional campus that has reoriented its mission around the needs of Portland as a city. Its mission has a specific regional and urban focus:

> *The mission of Portland State University is to enhance the intellectual, social, cultural and economic qualities of urban life by providing access throughout the life span to a quality liberal education for undergraduates and an appropriate array of professional and graduate programs especially relevant to metropolitan areas. The university conducts research and community service that support a high quality educational environment and reflect issues important to the region. It actively promotes the development of a network of educational institutions to serve the community.* [Portland State University, 1999, http://www.pdx.edu/psumission.phtml]

This mission is enacted through faculty and student involvement in service-learning, continuing education, applied research, lecture series on topics relevant to the community, and other types of community-focused events.

Urban comprehensive and regional universities occupy a unique place in the comprehensive system and the engagement movement. "Urban institutions have committed themselves to helping solve [these] urban problems as part of their service mission" (Crosson, 1983, p. 49). Many urban campuses have embraced their place in the community as change agents (Brown, 1994; Mayfield, Hellwig, and Banks, 1999). Through the work of the Coalition of Urban and Metropolitan Universities, in particular, there has been focus on the unique place that urban regional campuses play in the higher education landscape. This is not to suggest that other institutional types are not part of urban problem solving. All urban campuses, whether they are community colleges or elite research universities, have considered their role in community renewal and have looked to their civic mission as a way to address urban problems (Braskamp and Wergin, 1998; Crosson, 1983, 1985, 1988).

Liberal Arts Colleges. Congruent with the missions and history of liberal arts colleges, (re)focusing on service has meant capitalizing on the close community and campus relationships that already exist (Fear and Sandmann, 1998). Especially in small, rural communities, the presence of a campus is central to community vitality, both historically and currently (Potts, 1977). Just as with internal service, external service on many (if not most) liberal arts campuses is central to the vitality of the campus.

In many ways, linking learning and community service builds on the particular strengths of small, independent liberal arts colleges. Most include service as part of their mission. For many church-related and Christian colleges, developing a service lifestyle is one of their core values. Many students have developed a strong service motivation in their churches and communities prior to entering college. Scholarship at small colleges is already defined broadly and includes interdisciplinary approaches to issues (Boyer, 1990). Teaching and student learning are central (Eby, 1996).

Involvement in external service, and especially service that supports local concerns, is a natural extension of campus positionality (Votruba, 1996). Furthermore, the focus on student learning, undergraduate research, and interdisciplinary studies that exists on most liberal arts campuses makes for a natural segue into service-learning, which can serve all of these foci. Close relationships between campuses and communities that already exist are natural mechanisms for connecting faculty and students with community needs. The external service and outreach of liberal arts colleges are resources for addressing community issues (Eby, 1996).

Many liberal arts colleges are residential in nature. The close relationships between faculty and students in a residential setting, in addition to the focus on liberal arts education, offer additional opportunities to expand teaching and service beyond the classroom (Prince, 2000). "Residential liberal arts colleges have an unequaled potential within higher education to integrate knowledge and action in a holistic educational community" (Prince, 2000, p. 258). An example of how a liberal arts college builds on both its service mission and residential nature is Wartburg College in Iowa. Wartburg students can choose to live in residence halls with a service focus. As part of the living and learning experience, students extend classroom learning into community settings by making a commitment to service as part of their living arrangements.

Many liberal arts colleges are also faith related; they have relationships with religious authorities of a particular church that give these campuses a distinct spiritual and religious character. This is not to suggest they are all owned and operated by a church; most campuses maintain institutional autonomy and academic freedom (Byron, 2000). Faith-related higher education has been successful in initiating and maintaining community partnerships. In fact, religious-based campuses have higher numbers of students participating in service activities than students at other types of campuses (Byron, 2000). "Inescapably, the faith-related college or university, as citizen actor and as institutional educator of the young, lives in overlapping spheres of influence: academy and community, faith and reason, town and gown, mind and matter" (Byron, 2000, p. 293).

National associations of liberal arts colleges have been instrumental in encouraging community service, service-learning, outreach, and community partnerships at and among liberal arts schools. In many instances, the focus on service is not a new concept, but instead represents a new emphasis on old priorities (Fear and Sandmann, 1998). For example, over the past ten years, the Council of Independent Colleges has maintained a leadership position in renewing the civic mission of member institutions through the Engaging Campuses and Communities project and other grant projects to support service-learning. In addition, the Associated New American Colleges, a coalition of liberal arts–focused colleges and universities, has developed a new academic compact between faculty and their institutions as a means to reinvigorate faculty service.

Research Universities. Policies, procedures, and practices at research universities affect what other campus classifications do and how they do it (Checkoway, 1997). Research universities are a formative force in setting standards for all of higher education (Geiger, 1999). They have a unique role in generating norms for academe in general and for the academic profession in particular since it is research universities that "prepare the professors who populate the nation's colleges and universities" (Checkoway, 2001, p. 126). These universities individually and collectively have taken a leadership role in the service movement (Butler, 2000).

From an empirical standpoint, research by Rowley (2001) indicates that research universities, in comparison to other institutional types, are more likely to have public service programs, official definitions to support public service, institutes or centers to support outreach, and institutes or centers that do the same. This is not surprising, given the land grant tradition that exists within many research universities; the ideal of service is central to the history of these campuses.

However, research universities are also the first to be criticized for losing sight of both teaching and service missions in the face of mounting demands related to research (Boyer, 1990; Boyte and Hollander, 1999; Kennedy, 1997; Lagemann, 1991). The American research university is criticized for being out of touch, not serving community needs, and losing sight of its civic purpose (Boyer, 1990; Boyte and Hollander, 1999; Butler, 2000; Checkoway, 2001). Much of this criticism centers on the belief that research overshadows other priorities and missions (Gamson, 2000). In addition, research universities and their myopic focus on research can influence other campuses that aspire to drift upward and emulate the research institutions (Aldersley, 1995; Finnegan, 1993; Morphew, 2002). The emphasis on research is congruent with the mission of the research university and is therefore appropriate. Research plays an important role in meeting society's needs for knowledge (Walshok, 1995, 1997, 2000). The problem lies in a singularity of purpose that has emerged with regard to research activities (such as grant acquisition and publications) and how this focus affects other aspects of the research university mission. Thomas (1998) argues that "colleges and universities are not ignoring their civic responsibilities, but they could be taking them more seriously" (p. 3).

Research universities offer some of the greatest resources for civic renewal and house some of the strongest voices for renewal of the civic role of universities (Butler, 2000; Checkoway, 2001). The literature is replete with examples of research universities and their attempts to reclaim their civic missions (Keener, 1999; Ray, 1998; Spanier, 2001; Walshok, 2000). The National Association of State Universities and Land-Grant Colleges (NASULGC) has been one of the most vocal and organized leaders in the movement to reform higher education and has called on state and land grant universities, in particular, to reclaim their "vital roles in economic and social development" (Magrath, 1999, p. 3). Much of the work of NASULGC has been supported by the Kellogg Foundation to examine the future of land grant universities. The general intent of these initiatives is to focus on the overriding objective of serving the public through teaching, research, and service missions (Magrath, 1999). The Association of American of Colleges and Universities, American Council on Education, Association of American Universities, American Association for Higher Education, and Campus Compact have all been instrumental in addressing the past, present, and future civic roles of the American research university.

Special-Focus Colleges. Special-focus colleges and universities are those dedicated to meeting the unique needs of particular ethnic minority groups (for example, tribal colleges). Although not an institutional type unto themselves in the Carnegie Classification sense, special-focus colleges have played a unique role in the outreach movement. As a campus type, the special-focus colleges warrant consideration here given their long tradition and history in support of community service and outreach. Historically black colleges and universities, in particular, have a very long and strong orientation to civic involvement (Ayers and Ray, 1996; Scott, 2000). About historically black colleges, Scott (2000) writes, "In short, the institutions were expected to provide direction, training, and opportunities to practice civic engagement and community building, such as cooperative programs for building houses and shelter for families" (p. 264).

Tribal colleges, historically black colleges and universities, and Hispanic-serving institutions tend to be located in ethnic communities. The relationships that exist between these communities and the campuses supporting them are unique. For example, "tribal colleges, like the larger Native American communities in which they dwell, are deeply rooted in an ethic of service. The concept of neighbor helping neighbor is part of life on both the reservation and in tribal colleges" (Ward and Wolf-Wendel, 2000, p. 772). Special-focus colleges exist to meet the needs of their communities in unique and specific ways that are typically absent on other types of campuses. The historically black colleges exist to meet the needs of the African American community. Furthermore, special-focus colleges educate the citizens "of whom a significant percentage come from the community often targeted for community service and service-learning" (Ayers and Ray, 1996, p. v). These dynamics and others merit special consideration of special-focus colleges. Additional research is needed regarding how service roles are enacted on special-focus college campuses.

The Perspective of Institutional Type. In sum, viewing outreach and engagement and accompanying service activities from the perspective of institutional type shows an interesting variation in purpose and definition. The types of external service in which faculty are engaged are shaped by institutional type and the expectations for involvement beyond the campus that emanate from the campus. Institutional diversity is important to higher education and in particular in the area of service. The literature makes clear that campuses are distinct based on their missions and how these missions are enacted. In the area of service, campus missions are particularly important as to how campuses view themselves as part of the community. The diversity of the American higher education system is one of its greatest strengths. This diversity benefits society by providing education that meets certain niches. In the area of service, institutional diversity benefits society as campuses uniquely approach the ideal of engagement.

> If mission is the defining characteristic of classification and public service is a key component of mission, then service must be considered along with campus commitment to teaching and research.

Including Public Service in Classification Systems. Recently, attention has come to including public service in the Carnegie institutional classification systems (Church, 2001; Holland, 2001; McCormick, 2000). If mission is the defining characteristic of classification and public service is a key component of mission, then service must be considered along with campus commitment to teaching and research. In classification systems such as Carnegie, "Revisions are needed to take into account a greater diversity of institutional interpretations of academic mission, faculty roles, and institutional priorities" (Holland, 2001, p. 1). Current conversations about the Carnegie Classification of colleges and universities are under way to consider ways to capture in future classifications the distinctiveness and variability that exist in how institutions define themselves (Church, 2001; McCormick, 2000).

Discipline

Not only is outreach defined and interpreted by campus type, it is also affected by discipline. Disciplinary norms, more so than institutional norms, are key for determining how faculty carry out their work (Clark, 1987). Disciplines have a major impact on faculty priorities (Clark, 1987; Diamond and Adam, 1995; Rice, 1996b; Zlotkowski, 2000, 2001). A professor of nursing is likely to approach the task of outreach differently from the professor of medieval history, based on job descriptions, classes taught, and research foci.

There are two issues to consider with regard to the disciplines and their impact on faculty outreach roles. The first is the role of disciplinary associations (as arbiters of the discipline) in encouraging and supporting faculty civic involvement and outreach (Diamond and Adam, 1995; Zlotkowski, 2000, 2001). For many disciplinary associations, service and service roles have not been a point of emphasis. As higher education as a whole has begun to focus on service and engagement, so too have the associations. To address this issue, some associations have shifted focus to the need and opportunity for disciplines and their members to be involved in community problem solving and social change. Examples include the work of the National Communication Association and the Modern Language Association, which have recently undertaken initiatives to examine the role of external service in faculty life.

The National Communication Association, through the Communicating Common Ground project, has focused on engagement as a way to get faculty, students, community groups, and K–12 schools to find ways to respect diversity and combat prejudice (Applegate and Morreale, 2001). The association has served as a conduit for partnerships with other organizations and as the impetus for campuses to participate in projects and secure grant funding. Another example is the work of a faculty committee of the Modern Language Association, which created the report *Making Faculty Work Visible* (1996). This report examines the role of teaching, research, and service and offers suggestions and examples that guide the conduct of faculty work. In addition, the American Association for Higher Education (AAHE) as an interdisciplinary professional organization has supported a monograph series on service-learning in the disciplines. The series has been instrumental in getting disciplinary associations to think about the significance of community-based work for disciplines in general, for faculty who are part of those disciplines, and for the associations themselves (Zlotkowski, 2000). In addition, AAHE, like many other associations in recent years, has dedicated conference themes to topics associated with service and engagement.

The second issue with regard to outreach and the disciplines is how different disciplines respond to civic involvement and its relative importance in faculty life. "Among all the subject matter differences that divide the professoriate, none are larger in the latter decades of the twentieth century than the sometimes gaping divide between professional schools and 'the basic disciplines'" (Clark, 1987, p. 93)

These professional schools—medicine, engineering, law, medicine, nursing, social work, public health, education, and agriculture—share the common characteristic of simultaneously having to combine practical and academic goals (Clark, 1987). Professional units have to deal with these tensions internally in terms of combining the practical and the academic, but also from a legitimacy standpoint as these units must adopt academic norms in order to meld into the larger academic milieu. The basic epistemological foundations (and differences) between professional fields and basic disciplines (arts and sciences disciplines) have a great impact on how outreach missions are defined and rewarded (Dinham, 1987). "Today's epistemologies have become complex, diffuse, inclusive, controversial, and not considered equally valid and valuable by all academy members" (Braskamp and Wergin, 1998, p. 83). Both within and among disciplines, conversations about basic differences in assumptions about knowledge and about researchers' relationship to knowledge acquisition abound (Wildman, 1998). Faculty involvement in outreach challenges basic assumptions about research versus practicality and basic scientific understanding versus applied research (Walshok, 1995, 1997, 2000). On some campuses, this creates alliances and on others tension.

The focus on the discipline is important. Much of the rhetoric of engagement has been focused at institutional levels, but it is at the disciplinary level that professors will reach out and engage their communities (or not). To change faculty attitudes and actions regarding engagement requires support for faculty where they work: in their departments (Eckel, 2000b). Institutional initiatives that are not backed up with administrative support for the departments often find that they lack the support of the departments, with predictable results: "Institutional mandates will, in most instances, founder on the rocks of departmental autonomy, and institution priorities may be less influential than disciplinary norms" (Zlotkowski, 2000, p. 310).

In professional schools, graduate and professional students are being trained to work in specific settings, generally outside the academy. In professional schools such as education, service is of central significance, and faculty are expected to be involved in external service (O'Meara, 2002; Oakes and Rogers, 2001). Expectations evolve from long traditions of service (Lawson, 1990) and apprentice models of socialization (Brubacher and Rudy, 1997). In addition, expectations evolve from professional necessity and the call for professional field faculty to develop an interface with the communities they serve (for example, for education faculty, schools; for social work faculty, social service agencies). For professional faculty to maintain awareness of the issues affecting their field, they must be engaged in that field through the myriad of outreach activities described here. Research in professional fields typically has an applied component. Unlike more esoteric scholarship that is an end unto itself, "exoteric" research is focused on meeting the needs of specific audiences. Research in this vein is conducted with specific audiences in mind, and those audiences extend beyond the campus (Lawson, 1990).

Traditional definitions of scholarship do not always suffice for faculty working to connect theory and practice through applied research (Lawson, 1990; Oakes and Rogers, 2001). Traditional and segmented notions of teaching, research, and service are insufficient to explain and reward the interdisciplinary, collaborative, and applied research that emanates from professional schools. Furthermore, not all institutional types or disciplines value applied research and the research that can emanate from doing research tied to service and service-learning (Kezar and Rhoads, 2001). Outside schools of education, classroom-based research to assess the effectiveness of service-learning in a class or series of classes may not be considered favorably at certain research universities because it is based on pedagogy and not on advancing the discipline. In addition, research that emanates from service projects (for example, a report of an evaluation for a state agency) would not be considered "real research," because, when subjected to normal indicators of rigor in research universities, it fails on the basis of the referee process and publication venue. Research is made complex by outreach. Disciplines and institutional types are likely to value the work of outreach differently.

The University of California, through the work of a committee to look at schools of education and their relationship with the community, suggests the need for new ways to evaluate scholarship emanating from professional schools (Oakes and Rogers, 2001). Traditional basic research by its definition is disconnected and based on tenets of objectivity. Much of the research generated by scholars at professional schools is applied research. These scholars can find themselves in a bind: their campuses may require traditional research for promotion and tenure, while their profession may require work more directly addressing the needs of the community served by the profession. At the University of California, the panel suggested that the work of professional schools be judged by new structures that support applied research as well as more esoteric, basic research (Oakes and Rogers, 2001). Such a process would judge research based on the values and standards of the field and not so much by the values emanating from arts and sciences models of research.

Outreach keeps professors in touch with developments in their field. Higher education practitioners, particularly in professional schools, need to maintain connections with the realities of the workplace for which they are preparing students. A professor of business works with students who will be entering dynamic, changing fields. If these professors do not adapt their curricula to changing conditions, they poorly serve their students. Faculty outreach and service provide a means for professors to stay connected with the communities they serve, allowing them to keep their teaching material and their research more up-to-date, responsive, applicable, and relevant (Friedman, 1993; Lawson, 1996).

There are also empirical data about faculty involvement in service by discipline. Antonio, Astin, and Cress (2000) found that faculty members in education, health sciences, ethnic studies, and social work—fields associated with the improvement of people and communities—were the most committed to community service. Disciplines least likely to be involved in or supportive of outreach initiatives were math and computer science, foreign languages, physical sciences, anthropology, and English.

Demographics

Another aspect of difference that relates to faculty external service roles is tied to personal demographics and, in particular, race and gender. Antonio and others (2000) found that women, nonwhite faculty, and lower-ranking faculty tend to be most involved in community service. A recent study by O'Meara (2002) also found that women and nonwhite faculty are disproportionately represented among those who are involved in what she identifies as service scholarship.

There has been increasing attention to the added responsibility that faculty of color face in predominantly white college settings in terms of internal service responsibilities (Aguirre, 2000; Baez, 2000; Padilla, 1994; Tierney and Bensimon, 1996; Turner, 2002; Turner and Myers, 2000). This imbalance also applies with regard to external service. Consider, for example, the sole African American on the faculty who is a prominent member of the community at large and active in the discipline. This hypothetical faculty member, a member of the social work department, is asked by his department to be on two search committees for contributions he can make to attract minority candidates and to help monitor the committee in terms of diversity. Based on his community involvement, he is also asked to be on the board for a new boys' and girls' club in the community. In addition, he has been asked to chair the ethnic diversity committee of a national social work association. These involvements are based on his expertise as a social work educator and researcher, in addition to his ethnicity. For the lone African American faculty member in a department, and especially a department or campus with a commitment to diversity, this service in the name of representing ethnicity can be taxing in terms of time and in terms of activity that can be perceived as marginal (Aguirre, 2000; Padilla, 1994; Tierney and Bensimon, 1996).

Rarely are white faculty called on to represent their ethnicity. This is not to say that white faculty members are not called on to fulfill service responsibilities, but that faculty of color and women in male-dominated departments can be called on doubly to fulfill service roles to meet the needs of their departments *and* to fulfill service obligations that meet the needs of their race or gender (Aguirre, 2000).

Racial uplift, a concept explored by Perkins (1997), places communal concerns above those of the individual and of the institution. Perkins in her research asserts that the purpose of education for some black women is not a matter of self or institutional improvement, but rather a means to improve their race—what she calls race uplift. Although her work focuses on the differences of education for black and white women in higher education, her findings can be extended to faculty. The concept of racial uplift situates individuals as members of communities and sees those individuals seeking education "to assist in the economical, educational and social improvement of their enslaved and later emancipated race" (p. 184). Racial uplift is a concern for students and faculty. Involvement with external racial communities through service is an important mechanism for faculty and students to contribute to their racial community (Harris, 1998).

> **For faculty of color, there are constant decisions every day between obligations that are focused on individual accomplishment, such as publishing a research article, and obligations to their racial or ethnic communities.**

For a faculty member, a conflict can arise between racial uplift goals of working to improve and advance the condition of one's race and promotion and tenure obligations that discourage outreach activities in favor of more solitary pursuits like research and publication (Townsend and Turner, 2001). Certainly, faculty can have societal and community impacts through their research, but for faculty of color, there are constant decisions every day between obligations that are focused on individual accomplishment, such as publishing a research article, and obligations to their racial or ethnic communities, or what Baez (2000) calls "race-related service." He notes that many minority faculty feel "compelled or driven to participate in activities they believe would benefit their racial or ethnic communities" (p. 374). The pressures are both internal and external. Faculty of color who find themselves as sole representatives in their departments can face internal pressure to advise minority student groups or participate in every search, knowing that otherwise their perspective may not be included. External pressures can come from community members both on and off campus who expect educated and successful people to help lead and contribute to the betterment of the race community.

The overrepresentation of women and minority faculty in service involvements has a few interesting twists. As long as faculty who are on the margins (adjuncts, faculty of color, women faculty) are supporting community service initiatives, then community service initiatives will stay marginalized (Antonio and others, 2000; O'Meara, 2002). Furthermore, as long as service is marginalized and underrewarded in the academic work hierarchy, faculty who are extensively involved in service will risk the ultimate marginalization: denial of tenure for failure to engage in the activities that are rewarded through promotion. The dilemma that those who serve often lose the privilege of serving presents a challenge for scholars interested in their service roles and campuses interested in creating a service culture. As long as service occurs among enclaves of scholars, and these enclaves are made up of marginalized scholars, the central culture of the campus is likely to remain unchanged (Singleton, Burack, and Hirsch, 1997).

Campuses are certainly opening themselves to the scholarly contributions that service activity can make, but there is still a long way to go in terms of elevating scholarship that is tied to service to the same level as traditional scholarship. This is particularly true at research universities, where research continues to be the primary indicator for success (Cuban, 1999). At other institutional types as well, there is still uncertainty about the relative importance of teaching, research, and service. All faculty, and minority faculty in particular, need direction and clarity to negotiate the fine lines of participation in particular activities that will lead to success as a faculty member. There will continue to be retention problems with minority faculty as long as they see helping their communities and doing their jobs as mutually exclusive.

Honoring outreach and illustrating how it can be tied to disciplinary expertise might be a way to bring minority faculty into the fold and have them use involvement in service as a bridge to success. This idea connects to Baez's (2000) notion of critical agency, which suggests that when service is used to redefine institutional structures, it can lead to changes that ultimately contribute to organizational change and social justice (that is, developing new promotion and tenure guidelines that value service). Outreach and work with communities is a way to integrate academic roles and avoid "conflicts of commitment" (Townsend and Turner, 2001). Integrated views of work where research expertise ties to community involvement that informs teaching is a way for faculty of color to transcend the dilemmas associated with compartmentalized views of faculty work. In the meantime, institutions need to continue to find ways to value faculty for the unique contributions they make to community and campus improvement.

The critical tensions that exist for minority faculty with regard to external service epitomize the tensions that exist for all faculty as they look to realize personal goals and campus missions tied to outreach, when the academic reward structure is just beginning to acknowledge the need to recognize and reward internal and external service. Members of the academic community need to "question the underlying assumptions that ensure that service is deemed inherently less valuable than those other criteria" (Baez, 2000, p. 364). By expanding the discussion from defining faculty service roles to thinking about how these roles might be recognized and rewarded, higher education can begin to function more effectively by encouraging faculty internal service efforts and supporting external service efforts to engage communities beyond the campus.

Linking Service to Scholarship

T HE PROSPECTS FOR DOING faculty work and doing it well can be daunting. Faculty responsibilities and workloads continue to expand. What faculty members decide to do with their time in any given day, semester, phase of career, or lifetime is shaped by multiple forces. Faculty service, internal and external, is but one of many things vying for faculty attention. Diamond (1999), in the work he has done on faculty evaluation, the need to document expanded notions of scholarship, and how faculty work varies by discipline (Diamond and Adam, 1995), illustrates the multiple factors that influence academic work. Figure 1 demonstrates how the faculty member and his or her work stand at the center of a swirl of activity and interactions with internal and external forces, including internal and external service. Diamond and Adam (1995) describe these factors as follows:

> *Department/School/College Assignments. Perhaps the most obvious factors that influence how faculty spend their time are formal assignments. Faculty assignments can be thought of as an outgrowth of institutional priorities enacted at the school/college and departmental levels. These might be imposed on or negotiated with the faculty member.*
> *Criteria for Faculty Rewards. A second set of variables affecting how faculty spend their time resides in the formal or informal statements outlining the criteria that will be used for making promotion, tenure, and merit pay decisions. Faculty understandably devote their time to activities that promise payoff for them.*

FIGURE 1
Factors Influencing What Faculty Do

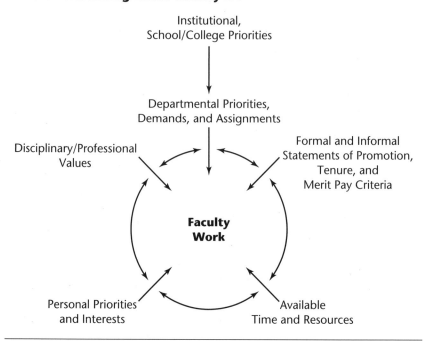

SOURCE: Diamond and Adam (1995), used with permission

Available Time and Resources. Time is a crucial variable for faculty. The academic calendar presents both a condensed year and many responsibilities competing for the same block of time. Public opinion to the contrary, most faculty work long hours. Workload studies reported in November 1992 note that faculty, on average, work more than 50 hours per week (Russell in Diamond and Adam, 1995). Time is finite, and the demands are many. One of the greatest challenges faculty members face is determining how to spend their relatively few discretionary hours.

Personal priorities. The personal priorities and interests of a faculty member are the fourth set of variables affecting faculty work. Given a choice, faculty will gravitate toward work in which they find pleasure and fulfillment [Diamond and Adam, 1995, p. 8].

Throughout this monograph, I have described these and other influences on faculty work with particular attention to how they affect faculty involvement in service roles. These additional influences, many overlapping with Diamond and Adam's work, include contemporary contexts; history, tradition, and mission; demands for internal and external service; institutional type; discipline; rank; and demographic characteristics. It is important to consider these factors given the ambiguous nature of service as something that can be "imposed on or negotiated with" faculty (Diamond and Adam, 1995, p. 8). Although there are certain internal service responsibilities that are integrated into faculty job descriptions (such as program coordination and committee work), external service responsibilities are likely to be less clearly defined, as they are highly variable based on mission, institutional type, discipline, and personal interests.

Expectations regarding faculty service, and in particular external service, are increasingly more commonplace in faculty evaluation standards (Lynton, 1995; Driscoll and Lynton, 1999). The application of these standards remains ambiguous on most campuses, even those with espoused values of outreach. There are many ways faculty can enact outreach—some active and some passive. Some faculty consider simply educating students to be a public service. This is a passive approach to enacting faculty service. In contrast, the faculty member who regularly uses service-learning and is involved with student projects in the community is enacting external service roles actively. Although it may be true that both of the examples contribute to the good of society in some way, the spirit in which outreach and service are being discussed is based on faculty enacting the roles actively. External service calls for direct interaction with audiences beyond the campus. Internal service calls for making meaningful connections on campus and in the discipline.

In the past fifteen years, considerable attention has been given to redefining faculty work in ways that reflect the complexity of what faculty do. Many of these conversations have centered around scholarship and the need to redefine what faculty do in ways that correspond to institutional and societal needs (Lynton, 1998; Votruba, 1996). The culmination of this thinking came with Boyer's now classic report *Scholarship Reconsidered* (1990). Boyer's work obviously struck a chord with institutions and their faculty. His work is not only cited regularly in the research literature; it has also become the foundation of numerous campus efforts to redesign reward structures around expanded definitions of scholarship (Braxton, Luckey, and Helland, 2002; Eby, 1996). Although it is difficult to state empirically how many campuses are engaged in redefining scholarship and rewriting promotion and tenure guidelines accordingly, few campuses have not been affected by the Boyer model and by other conversations that question the relative importance of the different aspects of faculty work and how this work ties to the mission of the campus (Braxton, Luckey, and Helland, 2002).

The one-size-fits-all model of scholarship (that is, traditional research) does not fit the workload demands of many faculty on the nation's campuses today (Diamond, 1999; Fairweather, 1996; Gamson, 1997; Leslie, 2002; Lynton, 1998). Faculty discontent, institutional concerns about myopic promotion and tenure guidelines, and a discontented public who see faculty work as out of touch have led to the creation of task forces on campuses throughout the country, culminating in new reward structures and new definitions about scholarship. Boyer's model expands and redefines what it means to be a scholar. His work is significant for what it offers campuses looking to redefine scholarship in ways that reflect the totality of faculty work and connect faculty work with institutional goals, missions, and objectives (Braxton, Luckey, and Helland, 2002).

Boyer did not work in isolation. His work was both a culmination of and a catalyst for thinking about scholarship and its meaning by different scholars questioning what it means to be a scholar and to do scholarly work. Eugene Rice, Pat Hutchings, Lee Shulman, and the late Ernest Lynton, to name a few, have also been instrumental in initiating and maintaining conversations about faculty work in all its forms. In addition, several organizations have taken up the task of redefining scholarship. These include the Carnegie Foundation for the Advancement of Teaching, the American Association for Higher Education, Campus Compact, the Council of Independent Colleges, and the National Association of State Universities and Land Grant Colleges. These organizations, as representatives for campuses and interests, have initiated discussions about scholarship and its definitions, scholarship reconsidered, the scholarship of teaching, and, more recently, what is now being called the scholarship of engagement.

The ultimate goal of this chapter is to present a rationale for linking service and scholarship. To do this, I provide an overview of the concept of scholarship, the scholarship of teaching, and the scholarship of engagement. In addition, I address issues of assessment and motivation.

Definitions of Scholarship

The post–World War II era was a time of expansion for higher education, leading to what Jencks and Riesman (1977) refer to as an "academic revolution." For campuses, this meant unprecedented diversification, growth, and expansion. For faculty, the academic revolution meant a professionalization of the professoriat and the emergence of professional norms (Finkelstein, 1984):

> *National and regional meetings for each academic discipline and sub-discipline are now annual affairs, national journals publish work in every specialized subject, and an informal national system of job placement and replacement has come into existence. The result is that the large number of Ph.D.s now regard themselves almost as independent professionals like doctors or lawyers, responsible primarily to themselves and their colleagues rather than their employers, and committed to the advance of knowledge rather than any particular institution* [Jencks and Riesman, 1977, p. 14].

Although Jencks and Riesman wrote this in 1977, much of what they were describing remains the case today. Indeed, some might argue that it is more pervasive today than in 1977. This view of faculty members as academic free agents rather than institutional, community, or academic citizens is behind the public perception that faculty have become unaccountable and unproductive. In part, this perception emerges from the very assumptions that shape what it means to be a scholar. These assumptions are articulated by Rice (1996a) as follows:

1. Research is the central professional endeavor and focus of academic life.
2. Quality in the profession is maintained by peer review and professional autonomy.

3. Knowledge is pursued for its own sake.
4. The pursuit of knowledge is best organized by discipline (i.e., discipline based departments).
5. Reputations are established in national and international professional associations.
6. Professional rewards and mobility accrue to those who persistently accentuate their specializations.
7. The distinctive task of the academic professional is the pursuit of cognitive truth [pp. 8–9].

This ethos of the academic revolution created a tradition of basic research that came to dominate what it meant to be a scholar, and the word *scholarship* came to be viewed as synonymous with basic research and publication (Caplow and McGee, 2001; Lynton and Elman, 1987; Paulsen and Feldman, 1995). For higher education, this has meant that graduate students are trained in a research setting, although only a limited number move on to research universities for employment. Graduate students as prospective and then new faculty recognize the need to take on teaching roles, but they still carry with them research norms shaped through graduate school experiences, regardless of whether the campus where they are employed has the same research orientation as the program from which they came (Austin, 2002; Cuban, 1999). This has two implications for faculty service roles. The first is for institutions hiring new faculty to be cognizant of the need to socialize these new members to institutional norms and expectations. If campuses want to integrate new faculty into service and teaching cultures (in addition to or in place of traditional research cultures), then the institutions must communicate their cultural values to the newly hired (Weidman, Twale, and Stein, 2001). In addition, if national discussions about "scholarship reconsidered" (Boyer, 1990) are to take hold and mold the profession into one that views different forms of scholarship as important, then graduate school experiences need to reflect these values (Austin, 2002; Richlin, 1993). For now, and until attitudes toward research and service change, graduate students will likely continue to focus on research as the currency that will get them into and then succeed in faculty positions. Although faculty work varies greatly by institutional type (some campuses take their teaching missions very seriously and do not require traditional research of their faculty), the norms that shape the profession as a whole tend to revolve around research.

Faculty overemphasis on research and publication limits the realization of campus and professional goals for teaching and service—the very heart of what higher education represents (Diamond, 1999; Gamson, 1997). The rise of the research university and the research orientation has had many consequences. "College instructors have become less and less preoccupied with educating young people, more and more preoccupied with educating one another by doing scholarly research which advances their discipline" (Jencks and Riesman, 1977, p. 13). Based on a study of disciplinary associations and their views on scholarship, Diamond and Adam (1995) found that in all types of institutions, "the present faculty reward system narrowly regards faculty work, and needs to be more inclusive in its consideration of the range of work faculty perform" (p. 13).

Faculty overemphasis on research and publication limits the realization of campus and professional goals for teaching and service—the very heart of what higher education represents.

While current occupation with Boyer's and other work that seeks to expand the definition of scholarship suggests that professional norms for faculty are starting to shift, it will take time for campuses to realize significant changes and for campuses to shift from a rhetoric that supports teaching and service to reward structures that support it (O'Meara, 2002). Clearly, academe in general, and faculty roles and rewards in particular, are in a state of transition, with increasing attention to expanded definitions of scholarship that include service and teaching in addition to research. Boyer (1990) states:

> *The most important obligation now confronting the nation's colleges and universities is to break out of the tired old teaching versus research debate and define, in more creative ways, what it means to be a scholar. It's time to recognize the full range of faculty talent and the great diversity of functions higher education must perform [p. xii].*

Boyer's message has been heard clearly throughout the country.

A shortcoming of Boyer's work, however, is that he never actually defines the essential elements that constitute scholarship. Faculty at Oregon State University, recognizing the importance of defining scholarship—its essential components and how it is applied—provide the following definition:

> *Scholarship is considered to be creative intellectual work that is validated by peers and communicated, including: discovery of new knowledge; development of new technologies, methods, materials, or uses; integration of knowledge leading to new understandings; and artistry that creates new insights and understandings* [cited in Diamond, 1999, p. 45].

What is important in this definition and relevant to the work put forth here is scholarship as creative intellectual work that is validated by peers and communicated. Diamond and Adam (1995) also contribute to the definition of scholarship, recognizing that

> *the weight given to any activity is highly context-specific; however, six features seem to characterize that work that most disciplines would consider "scholarly" or "professional":*
>
> * *The activity requires a high level of discipline-related expertise.*
> * *The activity breaks new ground, is innovative.*
> * *The activity can be replicated or elaborated.*
> * *The work and its results can be documented.*
> * *The work and its results can be peer-reviewed.*
> * *The activity has significance or impact* [p. 14].

In *Scholarship Assessed,* Glassick, Huber, and Maeroff (1997) put forward a set of standards that are specifically tied to Boyer's conceptions of scholarship as discovery, integration, teaching, and application. The standards were developed "to give the four kinds of scholarly activities the weight that each deserves" and to recognize and evaluate each as "scholarly acts" (p. 22).

Following is a summary of the standards:

Clear Goals
- Does the scholar state the basic purposes of his or her work?
- Does the scholar define objectives that are realistic and achievable?
- Does the scholar identify important questions in the field?

Adequate Preparation
- Does the scholar show an understanding of existing scholarship in the field?
- Does the scholar bring the necessary skills to his or her work?
- Does the scholar bring together the resources necessary to move the project forward?

Appropriate Methods
- Does the scholar use methods appropriate to the goals?
- Does the scholar apply effectively the methods selected?
- Does the scholar modify procedures in response to changing circumstances?

Significant Results
- Does the scholar achieve the goals?
- Does the scholar's work add consequentially to the field?
- Does the scholar's work open additional areas for further exploration?

Effective Presentation
- Does the scholar use a suitable style and effective organization to present his or her work?
- Does the scholar use appropriate forums for communicating work to its intended audiences?
- Does the scholar present his or her message with clarity and integrity?

Reflective Critique
- Does the scholar critically evaluate his or her own work?

- Does the scholar bring an appropriate breadth of evidence to his or her critique?
- Does the scholar use evaluation to improve the quality of future work? [p. 36]

These standards have been used by campuses to assess broadened definitions of scholarship. They are also helpful to lead campuses in discussion about the scholarship of engagement. As a tradition-bound institution, higher education has been reluctant to forgo traditional ways of evaluating faculty work (refereed publications and standardized teaching evaluations), leaving the questions: How do we evaluate engagement? Who will evaluate it?

What Diamond and Adam and Glassick, Huber, and Maeroff offer are assessment standards that define scholarship as an inquiry process that can be readily applied to teaching, research, or service. Their standards, and others developed from them, can be used to evaluate engagement and its scholarly attributes. This is not to say that all service, teaching, or research is scholarship or should be identified as such (for example, the professor using tired old lecture notes to teach a course is not engaged in the scholarship of teaching). The point to highlight is that the inquiry process can be extended to include service in much the same way it has been applied to research and, more recently, teaching: "Higher education's teaching and service performance will be strengthened, they [Boyer and colleagues] suggested, if faculty are encouraged to approach their work in classroom and community with the same care and curiosity that they bring to library, laboratory, studio, or field" (Huber, 2001, p. 22). In this way, scholarship as a process is one that can be applied to the complexity of faculty work. This is what has emerged for the scholarship of teaching.

The "who" question (Who will evaluate new forms of scholarship?) affects scholars who are concerned about being held to standards with which their reviewers are unfamiliar. In some instances, faculty are held to standards enforced or interpreted by faculty who never met those standards themselves. This has very much been the case on some research campuses where senior faculty, although productive, were not held to the same achievement standards as their junior faculty peers. A similar situation could happen with the scholarship of engagement.

Scholarship of engagement is in a period of transition and definition, and it can be difficult for faculty to trust a review process using new standards. The standards put forth above (Glassick and others, 1997) provide a framework to look objectively at a faculty member's scholarship as it may be linked to teaching, research, and service. Using new norms to evaluate scholarship calls for new ways to look at faculty evaluation. The transition from old norms of evaluation to new ones must be recognized as a process (O'Meara, 2002). To facilitate this process, California State University-Monterey Bay has faculty who will review dossiers go through a review session so they will know how to assess the scholarship of engagement. In addition, there is a new resource for campuses interested in external review of the scholarship of engagement. The National Review Board for the Scholarship of Engagement is composed of faculty from different disciplinary backgrounds and institutional types. These faculty are all active in the scholarship of engagement and have been trained to review dossiers. This board provides a resource to faculty whose campus peers and reviewers may not be aware of the scholarship of engagement.

Too often, service, in its myriad of forms, is viewed as mindless activity unrelated to the real work of the university or professoriat. For work to be considered scholarly in the academic context, it has to be viewed as intellectual and tied to faculty expertise. It is this grounding of teaching in the scholarly process (documented, reviewed, and disseminated) that has helped advance the scholarship of teaching. Edgerton, Hutchings, and Quinlan (1991) note that the scholarship of teaching, as with other types of scholarship, "relies on a base of expertise, a 'scholarly knowing' that needs to and can be identified, made public, and evaluated" (p. 1). There are certain underlying principles of scholarship that can be applied to all faculty functions. The scholarship of teaching relies on the use of the scholarly process to examine connections between pedagogical practice and content knowledge.

In the past fifteen years, the scholarship of teaching has gained increased visibility on college campuses and increased currency in promotion and tenure standards. It has taken a long time to gain legitimacy. Initially, the undervalued nature of teaching as a professional pursuit worried those who say teaching is a discipline-based scholarly act. The Carnegie Foundation for the Advancement of Teaching and the American Association for Higher Education have developed ways to assess the scholarship of teaching through portfolios, aided in adding teaching in a more visible manner to promotion and tenure standards, and started conversations on the scholarship of teaching on many campuses (Edgerton and others, 1999).

These efforts have legitimized the notion of a scholarship of teaching, moving it from a marginal to a more central place on many campuses. The scholarship of service is ripe for the same sort of evolution. Those parties interested in legitimizing a scholarship of engagement would do well to take note of the lessons learned in the press for more visibility and integration of the scholarship of teaching (O'Meara, 1997).

Scholarship of Engagement

At the 2002 meeting of the American Association for Higher Education Forum on Faculty Roles and Reward, Barry Checkoway (2002) defined the scholarship of engagement as "scholarship for the common good," where he contrasted the common good to the institutional good or the faculty good (other areas of faculty work).[1] He added that the scholarship of engagement (which Checkoway refers to as public scholarship) draws on the expertise of the discipline, makes connections with audiences beyond the campus, and connects the faculty career to the community. He identified the "prongs" of engagement as follows:

[1]There is much terminology associated with the concept of scholarship of engagement. Some refer to it as service scholarship (O'Meara, 2002), the scholarship of application (Boyer, 1990), professional service (Lynton, 1995; Driscoll and Lynton, 1999), public scholarship (Checkoway, 2002), or outreach or public service. I do want to acknowledge the different terminologies that exist to define the work that faculty do to extend their expertise beyond the campus. My use of the term *scholarship of engagement* is consistent with Boyer's work, and it also connects to current calls for the engaged campus. My choice in using *engagement* is tied to the reciprocal relationships implied in the term and with the larger work of the engaged campus.

- Reciprocity/community
- Reflection/stepping back/writing
- Common good
- Redefinition of research as tied to the public good
- Public scholarship, requiring new research methods
- Education for democracy
- Modified reward structures
- Change from the bottom up and the top down
- Cultural change in the profession

Elevating engagement to a level of scholarship on a par with research and teaching requires understanding and envisioning the faculty work of internal service and external service as intellectual activities. As faculty involve themselves in service, both internal and external, they need to do so in ways that tie their service work to disciplinary expertise or, as Lynton (1995) would have said, the knowledge enterprise. For faculty supporting internal service, this means lending expertise "as expert consultants and advisors to other faculty or administrators, applying professional expertise within the institution in a way that parallels external professional service" (cited in Lynton, 1995, p. 19). Internal service has the potential to be scholarly when it is treated in a scholarly manner (Ross, 1997). For example, the business professor with expertise in strategic planning who uses this expertise to guide the strategic planning process of his campus is enacting internal service roles that could be considered scholarship.

For faculty working to enact their external service roles, scholarship can be a more straightforward task, though not necessarily an easier one. The nutrition professor who helps the local food bank by bringing in students as service learners is naturally extending disciplinary expertise in the community. The challenge, then, is not so much serving the community as tying community work with disciplinary expertise in ways that will be recognized by campus reward structures. The challenge is applying the scholarship of

As faculty involve themselves in service, both internal and external, they need to do so in ways that tie their service work to disciplinary expertise.

engagement by planning, performing, evaluating, and reporting the service with the same depth, rigor, and curiosity as any other research or pedagogical project (Sandmann and others, 2000).

What we need today to move toward engaged scholarship is a "new fiction," to borrow the words of Rice (1996b, p. 572). This fiction would broaden tired and normative constructions of what it means to be a faculty member and would expand what it is to be a scholar and engaged in scholarship. "Scholarship properly communicated and critiqued serves as the building block for knowledge growth in a field" (Shulman, 1999, p. 5). Advancing a scholarship of engagement has implications for faculty roles and rewards. In addition, consistent with Shulman's notion of scholarship, it can serve to advance research and understanding in the meaning of engagement for faculty and the institutions where they work.

Boyer's scholarship of application is the most closely tied of his four scholarships (discovery, integration, teaching, application) to traditional notions of service. Boyer conveyed the need for scholarship to engage in meaningful societal problem solving. His work established links between the scholarship of application to faculty service. He was clear to define, however, that the scholarship of application was not about doing good and not about citizenship. The scholarship of application is not about civics but about scholarship. Boyer indicated that "to be considered scholarship, service activities must be tied directly to one's special field of knowledge and relate to, and flow directly out of this professional activity. Such service is serious, demanding work, requiring rigor—and the accountability—traditionally associated with research activities" (p. 22).

In the scholarship of application, Boyer (1990) saw a synergy between theory and practice: "Such a view of scholarly service—one that both applies and contributes to human knowledge—is particularly needed in a world in which huge, almost intractable problems call for the skills and insights only the academy can provide" (p. 23).

As an extension of the scholarship of application, Boyer later shifted to *scholarship of engagement* as a term to encompass the four scholarships of discovery, integration, teaching, and application and their ability to connect with needs that exist beyond the campus. I believe that Boyer's greatest cause as an educational theorist and practitioner was to address societal problems through education. Scholarship, which he had now reconsidered, was the way to bring the intellectual resources of the academy to make the world a better place for us all. Boyer (1996) saw the scholarship of engagement as a concept having two levels:

> At one level, the scholarship of engagement means connecting the rich resources of the university to the most pressing social, civic, and ethical problems, to our children, to our schools, to our teachers, and to our cities, just to name the ones I am personally in touch with most frequently. . . . At a deeper level, I have this growing conviction that what's also needed is not just more programs, but a larger purpose, a larger sense of mission, a larger clarity of direction in the nation's life as we move toward century twenty one. Increasingly, I'm convinced that ultimately, the scholarship of engagement also means creating a special climate in which the academic and civic cultures communicate more continuously and more creatively with each other, helping to enlarge what anthropologist Clifford Geertz describes as the universe of human discourse and enriching the quality of life for all of us [pp. 19–20].

The scholarship of engagement is not so much an addition to traditional scholarship as it is a way to use discovery, teaching, application, or integration to make a difference and to connect faculty with communities beyond the campus (Lynton, 1998; Votruba, 1996). Boyer offers an eloquent big picture and a sense of the urgency that we in higher education must use to make the work of the academy relevant and connected to community needs. Boyer's scholarship of engagement embraces all of the work of the university and its connection to the world around it. For Boyer, engaged scholarship meant that faculty as scholars were taking on world problems through disciplinary means, fulfilling campus mission, and incorporating teaching, research, and service.

Assessment and the Scholarship of Engagement

As many in higher education have taken to Boyer's notions about scholarship reconsidered in general and the scholarship of engagement in particular, defining the scholarship of engagement and determining how to assess it has become an area of increasing interest (Bringle and Hatcher, 2000; Bringle, Hatcher, Hamilton, and Young, 2001; Gelmon and Agre-Kippenhan, 2002; Driscoll and Lynton, 1999; Holland, 1997; Holland and Gelmon, 1998; Glassick, Huber, and Maeroff, 1997). The engaged campus movement in higher education has gained momentum, and Boyer's model of scholarship has gained currency on campuses throughout the country (Braxton, Luckey, and Helland, 2002). Folk wisdom has assumed that the scholarship of engagement is a good thing for higher education, but assessment is key for truly determining the impact and importance of engagement and the scholarship of engagement. Assessment is a necessary process for institutions to evaluate their engagement activities and measure their impact (Cambridge, 1999). "The scholarship of engagement includes the feedback of assessment as a basis for mutual improvement of academic and civic sectors" (Cambridge, p. 175).

Three aspects of assessment are germane to this discussion. First, assessment is used to determine whether an act of engagement represents a service activity (and if so what kind) and, further, to determine if the service performed is or can become a form of scholarship. This first type of assessment has been discussed previously in this chapter and has been the focus of the work of Glassick and others (1997). The second aspect is determining the level of campus involvement in engagement activities (Bringle and others, 2001; Holland, 1997). The third aspect of assessment is determining the impact the scholarship of engagement has on different constituents. Does the scholarship of engagement make a difference? For whom does it make a difference: community partners, faculty, students, the institution? These questions and others are the focus of calls for assessment.

As calls for engagement have surfaced, attention has been given to assessing institutional involvement to answer the question: To what extent are campuses involved? How do they communicate their commitment? Holland (1997), in an effort to analyze institutional commitment to service, developed a matrix that identified the key organizational factors that communicate commitment to service. The matrix is used to assess the level of relevance (level one to level four) of different indicators that communicate commitment to service (mission; promotion, tenure, hiring; organizational structure; student involvement and curriculum; faculty involvement; community involvement; campus publications). The intent of this assessment tool is for campuses to determine their level of commitment to different aspects of service. The focus here is on the institution (as opposed to the community or students or faculty).

Recognizing the complexity of assessing engagement given the range of stakeholders involved, Bringle and others (2001) have established instruments and processes by which campuses can simultaneously examine their own level of commitment and start to assess the impact of engagement initiatives. This approach identifies indicators that assess "the quality of activities, initial outcomes, and long-range outcomes for both the institution and the community" (Bringle, Hatcher, Hamilton, and Young, 2001, p. 90). This same group of researchers has established the Comprehensive Assessment of the Scholarship of Engagement (CASE) process as means to identify tasks that signal engagement (such as planning and resource allocation) and then analyzing these tasks relative to different stakeholders: the institution, faculty, students, and the community. This process allows a campus to assess its current level of involvement in engagement activities, including service-learning, and to assess future prospects. The Comprehensive Action Plan for Service-Learning (CAPSL) (Bringle and Hatcher, 2000) is another process whereby campuses can assess their engagement through focus on service-learning.

The Urban University Portfolio Project (UUPP) was developed as a way for selected urban universities to articulate the mission of the campus, a means of internal improvement, and a method to demonstrate effectiveness and accountability in the light of urban missions (Bringle and others, 2001). Although this model was developed specifically for the urban universities, all types of campuses can use it as an assessment tool. CASE, CAPSL, and UUPP are ways for campuses to identify the areas of civic engagement under way and to evaluate their effectiveness.

To date, the assessment conversation has been heavily focused on students and, in particular, the impact of service-learning on students (Eyler and Giles, 1999; Gray and others, 2000; Hesser, 1995; Kezar, 2002; Roschelle, Turpin, and Elias, 2000). It is important for higher education faculty and administrators to point to outcomes with regard to service-learning. In particular, Eyler and Giles have asked, "Where's the learning in service-learning?" To address this question, they relied on an analysis of existing research and conducted a national study to assess the impact that service-learning has on different aspects of student learning. Ongoing research attention needs to be paid to the outcomes and impact of service-learning (Boyte and Farr, 2000; Carpenter and Jacobs, 1994; Edgerton, 1995b; Ehrlich, 1999; Engstrom and Tinto, 1997; Hesser, 1995).

A challenge in assessing student learning is that service-learning as a pedagogical strategy is complex and that learning itself is complex. The outcomes of service-learning range from knowledge of academic content to increased civic engagement. "An underlying assumption of the national attention [to service-learning] is that community service-learning does in fact promote social and moral responsibility and provide other positive educational outcomes for undergraduate students" (Kezar, 2002, p. 15). Assessments of student outcomes need to capture the complexity of service-learning for its impact on traditional cognitive outcomes, civic and social responsibility outcomes, morals development, and cultural awareness. Narrowly defined assessment measures will be unable to capture this wide-ranging array of outcomes that service-learning can have (Kezar, 2002).

Several studies have been undertaken to see what impact service-learning has on learning (Eyler and Giles, 1999), moral development (Boss, 1994), and critical thinking (Astin and Sax, 1998). Generally, service-learning gets a good grade when it comes to seeing changes and positive impact on students. The research supports increased cognitive learning, moral development, and critical thinking as a result of service-learning. However, research needs to continue to explore dimensions like social responsibility and civic engagement, in addition to other aspects of learning and identity development. Additional research will continue to be important for assessing the impact that service-learning has on student outcomes.

The research supports increased cognitive learning, moral development, and critical thinking as a result of service-learning.

General assessment of the engaged campuses must continue to develop not just in terms of institutionalization of engagement and the impact it has on students; the assessment needs to extend to the larger societal context as well (Cambridge, 1999; Vernon and Ward, 1999). In the area of community engagement, which arises in part from public calls for higher education accountability, it is important for campuses to communicate how the efforts they are taking to further engagement benefit the community (Ewell, 1991; Gamson, Hollander, and Kiang, 1998). "The increased attention of state systems and individual institutions to assessment practices also makes clearly assessing and articulating outcomes from community service-learning [and other engagement initiatives] particularly important" (Kezar, 2002, p. 15). Assessment is tied to accountability (Ewell, 1991). Assessment and evaluation methods are necessary to demonstrate that engagement efforts are meeting their stated goals and to determine changes necessary for future activities. "Assessment information can affirm current practice or mandate change" (Cambridge, 1999, p. 176).

Assessment can also help to address concerns of critics of engagement and the scholarship of engagement. Critics acknowledge the spirit that informs discussions of engagement and service to the public, but they also question many of the assumptions behind the engagement movement. Is civic engagement the proper role for higher education? Is engagement paternalistic? Are educators and administrators truly interacting with their communities, or are they simply presenting the public with an academic agenda? Some of these questions are theoretical and philosophical. Others can be proved, disproved, or answered, and assessment of engagement activities and the scholarship of engagement provides a means to generate answers to some of these legitimate questions.

Faculty are the key players in helping campuses realize their goals for engagement.

Faculty Motivation and the Scholarship of Engagement

Faculty are the key players in helping campuses realize their goals for engagement. For the campus as a whole, reasons for pursuing engagement are many and clear: good public relations, active response to criticism, connection to historical mission, and positive involvement with surrounding communities. For individual faculty, however, the reasons for becoming involved in service activities that further engagement may be less clear. An analysis of research related to faculty motivation concerning involvement in scholarship of engagement activities reveals both intrinsic and extrinsic reasons.

Holland (1997) examined the factors that influence faculty involvement in public service (that is, external service) and found that faculty are mostly involved for intrinsic reasons, including personal values, a history of involvement, and a sense of personal responsibility. In short, Holland found that many faculty "engage in service because it is the right thing to do and because it allows them to link their personal and professional lives" (p. 38). Holland also found that faculty in certain disciplines felt more compelled to be involved in public service. For faculty in disciplines like nursing, social work, and education, involvement in public service activities is an inherent part of the position (Antonio, Astin, and Cress, 2000; O'Meara, 2002). Faculty in education, for example, may find it difficult *not* to be involved in public service activities due to the nature of the curriculum in certain departments. This stands in contrast to areas like philosophy, where faculty may not see apparent links with community audiences.

Faculty as members of a professional community may find that involvement in internal service both on campus and for the discipline is a way to belong and to feel a part of the academic community.

Finsen (2002) examined some of the intrinsic reasons that shape involvement in internal service. Involvement in shared governance is one way to improve on the academic condition, which for some faculty is in and of itself motivation to be involved. Faculty as members of a professional community may find that involvement in internal service both on campus and for the discipline is a way to belong and to feel a part of the academic community (Boice, 2000).

Another intrinsic motivating factor for faculty involvement in service is the good feeling that can come from seeing the impact of one's work in both internal and external realms (Wong and Tierney, 2001). Regarding internal service, faculty members who find their input on institutional decisions respected by administrators are more likely to value and participate in their internal service work (Finsen, 2002; Miller, Vacik, and Benton, 1998). Faculty can also find themselves motivated by the positive outcomes that come from service-learning to both students and communities (Hesser, 1995; Holland, 1997). Involvement in the scholarship of engagement affords scholars an opportunity to move beyond an individualized focus in ways that facilitate connection with campus, disciplinary, and local communities. In short, engagement activities provide faculty with a purpose, which for many is a powerful intrinsic motivator.

An obvious extrinsic reason for involvement in service is economic: job descriptions require it. But reward structures that value the complexity of faculty work, including the important contributions of internal and external service and scholarship of engagement activities, also can do more than require service; they can encourage it (Finsen, 2002). "Faculty understandably devote their time to activities that promise payoff for them" (Diamond and Adam, 1995).

Campuses that take seriously the goal of engagement need to reward their faculty for helping to realize institutional missions (O'Meara, 2002; Spanier, 2001; Ward, 1996). The institutionalization of service on some campuses has meant faculty development initiatives that reward service. These initiatives include fellowships, grants, release time, and cash awards for involvement in service (particularly service-learning and community-based research) and are a powerful motivator for getting faculty involved (Bringle and Hatcher, 2000). While rewards and awards are not always incentive for involvement in service, they help. Campuses can be proactive by providing recognition of service activities through promotion and tenure, establishing awards for outstanding service, and bringing attention to service activities. Furthermore, campuses with merit pay systems should include service fairly in these systems (Finsen, 2002; Sutton and Bergerson, 2001).

The distinction that can be attached to service can be an important extrinsic motivator for some faculty. At the disciplinary level, faculty involvement in service, particularly in regional and national associations, is shaped by opportunity for involvement with like-minded colleagues and the recognition and reward that come from this involvement (Clark, 1987). This is a concern, in particular, for newer faculty looking to establish themselves as scholars in the field (Finsen, 2002). Enhanced reputation can also be attached to external service as faculty work gets promoted in public venues. Many campuses have taken to highlighting faculty scholarship of engagement in campus publications as a way to communicate faculty who are at work meeting the needs of communities.

Scholarship of Engagement in Practice

The scholarship of engagement, like the scholarship of teaching before it, has captured the attention of many colleges and universities. Many campuses see the scholarship of engagement as way to elevate the importance of faculty work and tie it to community needs. For example, the University of Illinois, Chicago (UIC), in an effort to define the scholarship of engagement and its place in the reward structure, created a task force that produced a report defining the scholarship of engagement, making recommendations for how to reward it, and aiding faculty in making a case for the scholarship of engagement. The report provides specific directives for linking service to scholarship and for documenting it to fulfill needs for promotion and tenure evaluation.

This important document provides very specific and useful information to faculty about the scholarship of engagement: what it is, examples of it, suggestions for how to document it, and how to get rewarded for it. The document is also important because it is tied to promotion and tenure standards, and it stands in support of the campus Great Cities Initiative, an expansive initiative that represents UIC's commitment to Chicago as a whole and to neighborhoods adjacent to the campus in particular. As a research university, it would be very challenging for UIC to move beyond rhetoric in its service commitment if it did not have means to support faculty in their work directed to the campus mission of engagement. Similar processes of definition and accordant rewards have taken place at Michigan State University, Oregon State University, Portland State University, Otterbein College, and St. Norbert College.

Service need not be viewed, as it has in the past, as an aspect of faculty life devoid of or removed from scholarship. Faculty members who can extend their intellectual curiosity into their service activities, Huber (2001) suggests, can unify their professional lives, bringing together their teaching, research, and service in a synergistic way, to the benefit of each aspect of their work and the benefit of those they work with, both within and outside the university.

Faculty work has long been represented as comprising some specified proportions of teaching, research, and service, including academic citizenship and outreach. But when faculty take a scholarly approach to teaching and learning, or to service in its various forms, the boundaries between the conventional parts of academic life can easily blur:

> *The scholarship of teaching like the scholarship of engagement calls for viewing academic work as an integrated whole instead of as a series of distinct parts. To realize this goal for public scholarship and outreach calls for "rethinking old categories if the academy wants to produce new kinds and forms of knowledge and see them thrive" [Huber, 2001, p. 29].*

An Integrated View of Faculty Work

The engaged campus is one where the mission of the campus is committed to connecting the resources of the campus with needs that exist in the community (Sullivan, 2000). Engagement is a joint effort involving all members of the campus. Faculty are the foot soldiers of the engaged campus: administrators may set goals for the university, but the actual act of engaging with various communities is most often accomplished by professors. To fulfill the goal of engagement, scholars must link their teaching, research, and service to community problems, challenges, and goals, whether the community served is the department, the university, the town, state, or nation, or the global community. They must integrate their teaching with the needs of their students, their department and university missions, and the goals of their administrators. Finally, they must envision and enact their service roles, both internal and external to the university, to mean something more than sitting in meetings and generating memos so that higher

Engagement is a joint effort involving all members of the campus.

education can function more effectively internally, as a means to function more effectively externally (Berberet, 1999, 2002; Lynton and Elman, 1987).

To realize this vision of an engaged campus fully, an integrated view of faculty work is necessary. Without it, teaching will continue to stand in opposition to research and both in opposition to service. Professors will continue to feel that their service distracts them from their teaching and research obligations. A scholarship of engagement links a scholar's service to his or her expertise and links teaching, research, and service activities to one another. Connections among teaching, research, and service are what make engagement part of the mission of an institution (Singleton, Burack, and Hirsch, 1997).

In some ways, the idea of an engaged campus and an integrated view of faculty work harkens back to the birth of the land grant institution and the Wisconsin idea. Once again, we are talking about and searching for a way to take the expertise of scholars and address the needs of communities, although today we might define community even more broadly than before, to include communities both internal and external to the university. Where the scholars of the land grant era were encouraged to use their research to address the needs of a growing nation, a campus system pursuing engagement encourages professors to use their scholarship and expertise to address the needs of their students, departments, disciplines, campuses, and communities. Engagement encourages the synergy of teaching, research, and service, recognizing that the different parts of a faculty member's life can serve one another rather than pull in opposite directions. Huber (2001) notes that "faculty work has long been represented as comprised of some specified proportions of teaching, research, and service, including academic citizenship and outreach. But when faculty take a scholarly approach to teaching and learning, or to service in its various forms, the boundaries between conventional parts of academic life can easily blur" (p. 23).

It is easy to look longingly to the days of land grant institutions and the Wisconsin idea for what these ideas did for the service movement, but even then, the challenges existed that face us today: finding ways to encourage faculty to use their research to inform teaching and to use insights from both teaching and research to inform service. A synergy exists between the different components of faculty work, and the engaged scholar is one who can bridge and unify these components and then use that unity of knowledge and service to bridge the gap between the academy and the community.

For the higher education system to fulfill its mission, engagement with the communities that surround and support it is essential. Before the university can properly do the work of reaching out, however, the internal structures to support this outreach must be established (Bringle and Hatcher, 2000). In an effort to support engagement initiatives, campuses have established centers that provide a point of contact for faculty, students, and communities to interact. Although these centers have many different names (for example, Office for Civic Engagement or Center for Community Outreach), they tend to have a common mission: to facilitate campus and community connection through activities like service-learning, community-based research, and volunteerism (Gray, 2000). Faculty external service activities to support engagement are also often facilitated by teaching and learning centers that support service-learning and research centers that encourage community-based research. Campuses that take seriously their engagement missions have an infrastructure to support the work (Holland, 1997, 1999; Bringle and Hatcher, 2000; Hinck and Brandell, 2000; Ward, 1996).

Unless and until faculty members can pursue external service without jeopardizing their jobs and stature, faculty will be unlikely to extend themselves to realize administrative calls for an engaged campus. Internal policies and procedures will need to permit and reward external service, and these policies can be created only when faculty are free to pursue internal service activities—committee meetings, planning sessions, internal consulting—without worrying that they have set their research agendas and teaching interests impossibly behind.

Service is part of the definition of the faculty role, but in practice it is rarely seen as an integrated part of faculty lives. Rather, service is seen as something that must be performed in addition to or in lieu of the scholar's other work, viewed as more important or pressing. To realize the goal for the engaged campus means that faculty and their institutions need to overcome the challenges that exist in moving engagement to a more central spot on the higher education landscape.

Moving Toward Engagement: Policy Questions and Their Responses

IN 1983, AUSTIN AND GAMSON CONDUCTED a comprehensive review of the current state of the academic workplace. They identified the tensions that existed between teaching and research and identified service as an "afterthought" as reflected in the literature. The service function of faculty has been referred to as the "short leg of the three-legged stool" (cited in Boyer and Lewis, 1985). On most campuses, service continues to be the least understood and correspondingly the least rewarded of all of the faculty roles (Berberet, 2002; Boice, 2000). Faculty members attempting to integrate engagement into their workload face a dilemma, caught between administrative and public calls for engagement and academic reward structures that tend to devalue outreach and engagement efforts. Efforts to engage campuses with communities will remain unfulfilled without attention to this and other dilemmas that face campuses, faculty, and the service movement in general.

The intent of this monograph has been to offer definition and clarity to faculty service roles in the hopes that understanding will lead to change. There are compelling reasons to face the challenges and relish the rewards engagement is bound to bring. This monograph calls for a view of faculty work that is grounded in the scholarship of engagement, as a means to tie faculty disciplinary expertise to campus and community needs and to integrate the different aspects of faculty work.

Following are some policy questions and responses to the legitimate questions that arise about the scholarship of engagement:

- *Given the prevalence of research in many reward structures, isn't encouraging faculty to be more fully involved in "new" forms of scholarships irresponsible?*

New forms of scholarship, particularly the scholarship of engagement, offer scholars great opportunity to unify and expand their research and professional lives.

Unless and until promotion and tenure guidelines acknowledge the effort and achievements involved in new forms of scholarship, faculty will face the risk that their efforts to expand their scholarship will not be rewarded. New forms of scholarship, particularly the scholarship of engagement, offer scholars great opportunity to unify and expand their research and professional lives, and many faculty find the work intrinsically rewarding. But until the work of engagement is recognized and rewarded extrinsically in the form of promotion and tenure, scholars will be unlikely to embrace these new challenges (Driscoll and Lynton, 1999; Holland, 1997; Ramaley, 2000a).

Reward structures must reflect campus priorities. On campuses where the focus is on teaching, for example, reward structures need to support this commitment. On campuses that have embraced the rhetoric of engagement and recognized the need for and benefits of an engaged and involved faculty, faculty evaluation guidelines need to reflect these priorities (Spanier, 2001). To accomplish this task, further efforts to define and expand the scholarship of engagement and to inform administrators and faculty of its intrinsic value and future promise are necessary (Sandmann and others, 2000). "Administrators and professors accord full academic value only to the work they can confidently judge" (Glassick, Huber, and Maeroff, 1997, p. 5), and they cannot judge new forms of scholarship until they define, understand, and appreciate them.

Through faculty internal service, many campuses are starting to rework promotion and tenure guidelines in line with institutional missions that support engagement. For example, faculty at Portland State University are held to standards of the Boyer model, and updated promotion and tenure guidelines reflect this expectation. Faculty have successfully gone through the review process using the new standards. When determining their embrace of new forms of scholarship, they need to appreciate their institutional norms for relative weight of teaching, research, and service. In addition, faculty need to be savvy about how they present their work as the scholarship of engagement (Driscoll and Lynton, 1999; Driscoll, Sandmann, Foster-Fishman, and Bringle, 2000; Sandmann and others, 2000). This includes tying faculty work to the mission of the campus, being purposeful and planful in developing an agenda for work tied to the scholarship of engagement, and creating linkages between the different aspects of their work and between traditional scholarship and the scholarship of engagement (Gelmon and Agre-Kippenhan, 2002).

• *Doesn't service to the community perpetuate hierarchies that exist between town and gown? Does the scholarship of engagement make a difference in communities?*

Campus calls for service have been well meaning in efforts to bridge campus and community relationships. At its very core, engagement is about reciprocal communication and interaction with community partners, calling for a focus on campus and community partners as "we" in favor of "us" and "them" (Ward and Wolf-Wendel, 2000). Building community partnerships is important to fulfilling goals of engagement. Successful partnerships require mechanisms to regularly gather local input on community perspectives about community needs and partnership development (Maurrasse, 2001; Vernon and Ward, 1999). At Providence College in Rhode Island, concerns about paternalism and disconnectedness with community have been addressed by inviting community partners to participate in classes as team teachers and to join problem assessment processes. "When professional service is truly scholarly a two-way flow of knowledge exists, to and from the locus of application" (Lynton, 1995, p. 21). The community impacts of engagement activities also deserve ongoing attention. The institutionalization of engagement requires assessment mechanisms that constantly evaluate and question the impact service has on local communities (Bringle, Hatcher, Hamilton, and Young, 2001; Cambridge, 1999; Vernon and Ward, 1999).

• *Doesn't the call for the scholarship of engagement just mean more work? Is it really fair to ask faculty, and in particular tenure-track faculty, to do one more thing?*

Time studies indicate increasing workloads for faculty (Berberet, 2002). These studies also indicate that faculty spend more time on research and teaching than they do on service, not surprising given the relative importance of each category in faculty evaluation guidelines. There are two responses to time problems for faculty. One, advocated by Rice (1996a), is viewing the faculty career holistically, meaning that at different times in the career, emphasis would shift between faculty areas of work and institutional priorities. Boyer (1990) referred to the use of creativity contracts as arrangements for faculty to define their goals for specified periods of time. For example, to become established, a faculty member might focus on the scholarship of discovery through specialized research. After four or five years, the faculty member could focus more on interdisciplinary and integrated approaches to problems in the field. Such creativity contracts are a way for faculty to delineate different emphases at different times in their careers. These contracts can serve as a focal point for annual reviews and for more summative reviews as well. At Oregon State, faculty develop annual work plans that allow them to adapt their responsibilities according to institutional needs and priorities as well as available professional opportunities (Finsen, 2002). These approaches help faculty alter approaches to their work in ways that satisfy faculty and institutional needs.

For faculty to be meaningfully engaged in communities requires them to understand how to make connections between research and community needs.

The second approach to dealing with time concerns is using an integrated view of faculty work, where what professors do as teachers, researchers, and service providers is viewed interdependently (Cushman, 1999; Lynton, 1998; Votruba, 1996). A scholarly life, regardless of institutional type, discipline, or rank, calls for a balance and synergy between and among faculty roles. For faculty to teach effectively, they must be grounded in current knowledge and information and engage students meaningfully in this content. For faculty to have their research make an impact, their work needs to be applicable to multiple audiences. For faculty to be meaningfully engaged in communities requires them to understand how to make connections between research and community needs (Cushman, 1999):

> *The traditional way of thinking about university activities exacerbates, rather than solves, the delivery problem. For one thing, it promotes a win/lose situation, i.e., one function wins at the expense of one or more other functions. It also fragments university functions through "hardening of the categories." Such thinking leads to teaching, research, and service in discrete and unconnected ways. There is another way to think about universities; that is, in terms of the knowledge functions that it performs* [sic] [Fear and Sandmann, 1995, p. 112].

Thinking about faculty work in this manner requires movement toward a scholarship of engagement where faculty roles reinforce one another.

If administrators want their faculty to do the work of engaging the campus with the community, they need to recognize that this request reflects a shifting of priorities. If the service of outreach is not recognized and rewarded, then faculty are being asked to shoulder additional work—to add engagement to their already full workloads. If instead the importance of faculty service contributions is recognized, then these expectations will be integrated into promotion and tenure guidelines, increasing the relative importance of service to research and teaching. Furthermore, the scholarship of engagement can tie together a professor's teaching, research, and service. If the contributions arising from scholarship of engagement are recognized and understood, expectations for more traditional, basic research could be moderated.

• *Service work disproportionately goes to faculty of color and women (Antonio and others, 2000). How can we prevent faculty from feeling additionally taxed by service?*

Service burdens weigh especially heavily on minority and women faculty and particularly in environments where they find themselves underrepresented. Presumably, any calls for increased service will also fall disproportionately on these groups, making their efforts to succeed in academe even more challenging than they already are. There are two factors to address.

• First, higher education must acknowledge the cultural taxation that women and minority faculty face and find ways either to reduce this additional service workload or note the benefits to the university of the behind-the-scenes work of marginalized faculty. We need to uncover the hidden workload and either recognize or reduce it.

Second, as members of the academic community, we need to "question the underlying assumptions that ensure that service is deemed inherently less valuable that those other criteria" (Baez, 2000, p. 364). As noted throughout this monograph, academic service, both internal and external, is a crucial part of the makeup and functioning of the university. Contemporary calls for engagement have only increased the importance of and need for service. Once again, we must recognize the value of academic service and its potential to unify and expand faculty research and teaching, and reward this service appropriately. When we recognize the contributions to the academy of faculty service, we will see that service is not "inherently less valuable," and we will acknowledge the contributions of those who serve, particularly women and faculty of color.

• *Graduate students as prospective faculty are socialized to assume traditional research roles in spite of the myriad of calls for multiple roles and the varying realities of faculty life at different institutions (Austin, 2002; Rice, 1999b; Richlin, 1993). How is the professoriat supposed to change if new graduate students still come to campuses focused on research?*

There are two aspects that need response here: new faculty socialization and graduate school preparation. Emphasis on research, and devaluation of service, begins for faculty during graduate education, which tends to be singularly focused on research (Richlin, 1993). Graduate students are often told that they must curtail outside involvements to focus on their research and their studies. The message, in effect, is that social and service commitments compromise their ability to do the work of a scholar. It is little wonder, then, that a new professor would shy away from service responsibilities, particularly when she often receives further reinforcement that she must be productive in her early years on the tenure track if she hopes to see her career prosper. It is also not surprising that faculty, particularly junior faculty, do not consider new ways to think about their service requirements during their early years; they are just trying to get service requirements, and often teaching requirements, out of the way, to focus on research, publication, and grant procurement. Efforts to create a scholarship of service will need to address this fundamental focus.

Faculty socialization is a powerful force. Just as it has been used to create and support professional norms for research, it can be used to support professional norms for expanded forms of scholarship. As more scholars are successful at integrating service into their scholarship, through service-learning and the scholarship of engagement, understanding and recognition of the role of service in faculty lives will be passed on to graduate students and new faculty. Early socialization can help develop ways of thinking and working that will help new faculty establish service as a priority on par with teaching and research. This process can be aided by creating clear guidelines for new faculty and encouraging mentorship in the subtleties of service, through the efforts of senior faculty and faculty development workshops.

Early socialization can help develop ways of thinking and working that will help new faculty establish service as a priority on par with teaching and research.

Graduate schools, especially research institutions, need to rethink the preparation of their students as prospective faculty, recognizing that their graduates may not find themselves working in a research institution:

> *The training of future faculty has neglected to socialize them to models other than that of the research university. Some junior faculty that I have known have so internalized their training that they exert the kinds of demands upon themselves that forbid any activity outside of the classroom or labs. And their chairs and mentors may now aid and abet such dereliction of duty, fearful of giving bad career advice—or of losing a position to a negative tenure decision* [Burgan, 1998, p. 20].

Graduate programs need to provide students with the opportunity to learn about different faculty roles and different campus types. This can be accomplished through mentoring, job shadowing, classes about college teaching or the professoriate, and workshops on the realities of faculty work.

Job descriptions that clearly reflect institutional expectations regarding service will also help new faculty establish priorities for their work. Current academic priorities reward research, recognize teaching, and acknowledge service. If campuses begin to emphasize engagement, job descriptions and promotion and tenure guidelines will need to embody this new emphasis.

• *Is there a way to use involvement in service to regenerate people's careers? Who is supposed to do service?*

The scholarship of engagement provides additional opportunity for faculty to make contributions to their field in ways that stretch beyond traditional teaching and research roles. It expands definitions of what it means to be a scholar and can be a vehicle of career renewal and definition.

> *The notion of the complete scholar becomes a career objective that unfolds over a lifetime of scholarly work. Faculty would have the opportunity to grow and change over time, being basically competent in, and committed to, a broader conception of scholarly work. They would agree for a set period of time to concentrate on one aspect of scholarly work where there is a special passion, be evaluated on the basis of that agreement, but then, if personal interests and institutional needs shift, move to concentrating on another facet of one's scholarly capabilities. Over the seasons of the academic life, a faculty member could become a complete scholar in the fullest sense* [Rice, 1996b, pp. 22–23].

Midcareer faculty tend to get lost in campus conversations about career development. There are workshops for new faculty to help them assume their roles and retirement seminars for helping people evolve out of their positions, but professors in the middle of their academic careers tend to get lost in the shuffle. Midcareer faculty are left on their own to negotiate what comes next. Rice's notion (1996a) of the complete academic is one way to view the faculty career. In this way, people can focus on different aspects of their career at different times (O'Meara, 1997; Rice, 1996a).

Faculty work is not static; it is dynamic and always changing (Diamond, 1999). Faculty who take on varied work roles lead more balanced (and presumably more professionally rewarding) lives (Boyer, 1990; Huber, 2001). As a nontraditional approach, the scholarship of engagement is a way for faculty to tie into new aspects of existing roles. Expanded views of scholarship provide new ways of encouraging generativity in mid- and late-career faculty. For the faculty member whose classes no longer inspire the commitment they once did, service-learning provides a means to try something new. If getting back into research seems daunting, connecting stalled faculty with community research projects might be a way to tap into their expertise in new ways. For others, engagement with communities beyond the campus may offer a way to feel less bound to the grind of research.

Expanded views of scholarship provide new ways of encouraging generativity in mid- and late-career faculty.

• *Service has so many meanings, and some service is viewed more legitimately than others. How do I know what counts? How should I spend my time?*

For a faculty member, the work that counts is ultimately the work that is rewarded, by retention, promotion, tenure, and monetary rewards. Faculty rarely know for certain which of their work activities are most important to their success or the relative weight of different work activities. This is true for research, teaching, and the myriad varieties of service. New faculty are often bewildered by the conflicting advice they receive regarding the need to focus on one or another aspect of their work. On some campuses, mission statements and promotion and tenure guidelines are clear road maps for a faculty career. At others, the junior scholar must try to balance the rumors and legends against the stated standards and then feel her way as best she can toward the goal of promotion or tenure.

Determining the relative importance of teaching, research, and service remains a challenge for almost all faculty members. Standards can be ambiguous, and they are subject to change over time. This has been particularly true in the area of service, which is usually referenced very generally in job descriptions and evaluation guidelines. The object of this monograph has been to help identify many of the types of service that faculty are called on to perform and the historical basis of that service in higher education. When administrators and faculty recognize that service is not monolithic, they can begin to be more specific by what they mean when they are discussing service: internal service, external service, civic and community service, service-learning, and service connected to a scholarship of engagement, for example.

- *Engagement, service, and outreach are all politically correct positions to take, and many presidents have embraced these concepts as ideals. How do campuses move from rhetoric to reality when integrating service?*

Contempoary calls for engagement are grounded, at least in part, by a need for higher education to be a better citizen. Some campuses have embraced this call in passive ways while others have been actively reconsidering their relationships with local communities.

> *American higher education is being urged from many sides to change that situation. It is being exhorted to turn the rhetoric of mission statements into the reality of an institutional commitment to direct interaction with public and private-sector constituencies, helping them to apply the latest knowledge and the latest techniques to the analysis and amelioration of their problems. And higher education must respond—but respond properly: by recognizing this kind of service as an integral component of its collective mission, and not leave it to individual faculty initiative* [Lynton, 1995, p. 9].

The rhetoric of engagement is compelling, and the engaged campus can meet many of the challenges discussed in the first chapter of this monograph. Engagement, however, will not arise solely from presidential proclamations and changes in mission statements. Faculty who are called on to make the engaged campus a reality will not undertake the efforts necessary if they worry that their institutions will not support them. If faculty fear poor evaluations and the denial of tenure because they have, at the urging of administration, shifted their focus from research to the service of engagement, they will soon enough abandon novel efforts at outreach and retreat to the relative comfort and stability of a career focused on research. Only when they know that the university's commitment to outreach and community involvement extends beyond rhetoric to reward will they accept and embrace a new outlook on service and engagement (O'Meara, 2002).

Faculty and administrators have to work in concert to support engagement. While individual faculty may adopt a scholarship of engagement without campus support (indeed many do), large-scale change requires simultaneous effort from the bottom up (faculty and students working for engagement) and the top down (administrators and boards supporting engagement) (Checkoway, 2002). These groups need to work together to determine how to use engagement to meet institutional mission, while remembering that the best way to encourage faculty involvement is with the carrot, not the stick:

Institutional reward structures provide the blueprint for how faculty spend their time. If an institution wants to be known for its teaching mission, for example, it must find ways of rewarding faculty for those activities that enhance teaching and student learning [Zahorski, Cognard, and Gilliard, 1999, p. 7].

Similarly, if an institution wants to be known for its commitment to engagement, it must find ways of rewarding its faculty for their efforts to make engagement a reality.

Recommendations for Research and Practice

COLLEGE CAMPUSES HAVE BEGUN to look for ways to address concerns, raised both inside and outside the academy, that our nation's higher education system is failing the citizens and communities that support it. One response to these challenges has been a call for colleges and universities to engage the world around them, working to extend and fulfill the mission of higher education to serve the community. This notion of an engaged campus sees all aspects of a campus working together for both the good of the campus itself and the good of the communities with which it interacts.

A major aspect in the creation of an engaged campus is the extension and enrichment of faculty service activities to perform the work of engagement. This monograph has examined the historical basis of the service functions of faculty work and how those functions have evolved as the nature of American higher education has changed. Other chapters examined aspects of faculty service roles in more detail, focusing first on the internal service that faculty perform for their institutions and then on the external service that they provide to support communities outside the university.

The research reviewed here makes a compelling case for the reason for engagement. Campuses are notoriously underfunded and constantly criticized. The reinvigoration of service is a way to respond to these problems. Several campuses from around the country have responded favorably, although campuses exhibit many different levels of integration of service into the work of engagement. Furthermore, integration of the scholarship of engagement calls for initiative at different organizational levels at the same time. Lessons learned by campuses that are attempting the work of engagement suggest several avenues for integration, including steps that can be taken by faculty, administrators, and the service movement in general.

For faculty, creating an environment where engagement can succeed means using internal service expertise and power to realize administrative promises about scholarship of engagement. Faculty have the resource of shared governance at hand. They can use this to develop working groups on engagement that take into consideration the mission of the campuses, in addition to unique challenges or opportunities to define and promote engagement. These working groups can establish definitions of service (internal and external) and how these tie to faculty work, provide examples of which activities count in each category of faculty work, and provide guidelines for assessment. Faculty need to develop workable guidelines that help fellow faculty and administrators know how engagement is being translated into faculty workloads and how it will be rewarded. Faculty at work fulfilling internal service roles can help develop structures that support external service roles. Conversations about faculty work need to take place among faculty in their immediate units and then campuswide. The work of Boyer (1990) and Glassick and others (1997) can provide catalysts for conversation about the role, scope, and implementation of engagement.

Faculty need to develop workable guidelines that help fellow faculty and administrators know how engagement is being translated into faculty workloads and how it will be rewarded.

For administrators, the scholarship of engagement presents many opportunities to awaken a campus to its past, present, and future. The scholarship of engagement is adaptable to all institutional types and all disciplines. For campuses with standards that are primarily focused on research, the scholarship of engagement can be used as a rubric to broaden definitions of scholarship that support teaching, research, and service missions. For campuses where teaching is the norm, the scholarship of engagement is a way to encourage faculty to rethink their teaching roles and add a scholarly component to teaching and outreach. This does not mean that all departments or campuses will embrace engagement or define it in the same way or that engagement will look the same from one unit to the next.

The administration must be clear about campus mission and the role that service and engagement play in this mission. Is there a clear call for service in the campus mission statement? How is it defined? Does the mission statement need to be rewritten? How does the campus use the mission statement? How does faculty work play in to it? How do students fit? How does the campus relate to the community? Campus conversations need to take place regarding the mission and scope of engagement initiatives. Campuses need to be aware about their ratio of lip-service to action. Are faculty being encouraged to do service and getting rewarded for it?

The scholarship of engagement is adaptable to all institutional types and all disciplines.

Has there been ample opportunity for faculty to have a voice in how the mission is shaped? Reorganizing (or further implementing) for engagement is an ideal opportunity for a campus to pause and consider its mission, tradition, past accomplishments, and future goals. The conversations can take place prompted by Lynton's (1995) "Ten Questions for Departmental Discussion," as well as Holland's (1997) matrix to assess institutional commitment and Furco's (2002) self assessment tool.

For the service movement in general, the world of engagement offers many opportunities. Calls for engagement have encouraged campuses to spring to action. It is heartening to see the number of campuses truly grappling with issues surrounding faculty work, varying definitions of scholarship, community relationships, and the meaning of service. Campuses have been inspired by the energy created around notions of engagement, service, and outreach. The engagement conversation needs to continue, and associations leading the discussion need to maintain momentum. There must be a conscious effort to include all institutional types and all disciplines in the conversation.

A review of the research and existing practice literature makes clear one thing: engagement is on the mind of higher education. Administrators are talking about it, faculty are grappling with it, and students want to be involved in it. Advocates of university service need to continue to bring new campuses on board, nurture campuses that are stalled, learn lessons from campus successes, heed warnings from campus challenges, and continue to find new ways to think about different notions of scholarship and how they tie to engagement.

Given the relative youth of the service movement on campuses, ongoing efforts are necessary to assess the impact that campus efforts have on their communities. From an empirical standpoint, it would be helpful to know if engagement makes a difference. Campus involvement in engagement operates at many levels, and future research needs to focus on different areas. Many compelling research questions have yet to be addressed.

Following are research questions, organized into different areas of operation and impact, to help shape a research agenda for engagement:

Faculty. Faculty are the key to a campus's integrating its service mission. Expanding faculty involvement in service is aided by knowing more about faculty and their involvements in service. Specifically, the following research could contribute additional knowledge about faculty involvement in engagement:

- How do faculty define service? Has this changed with administrative support of concepts like engagement?
- How do faculty talk about service? Do they see distinctions between internal and external service? How do they enact these roles? How do they define them?
- What policies and practices are in place in regard to consulting? Do faculty and administrators see consulting as a conduit for fulfilling service missions? How do campuses approach the issue of paid and unpaid consulting? How is consulting rewarded?
- Do campuses acknowledge the relative importance of different kinds of internal service? Are there opportunities for faculty to apply disciplinary expertise to internal service obligations? When does service end and administration begin?
- What are faculty perceptions about new forms of scholarship? Do they use them?
- How does faculty work vary by campus? How do faculty on different types of campuses value new forms of scholarship?
- Do faculty see involvement in the scholarship of engagement as a risky proposition or one likely to be rewarded?

Communities. From a research perspective, there has been embarrassingly little research informed by community perspectives of engagement. Future research needs to address this issue by addressing the following questions and others:

- How do communities define community?
- What has been the history of campus and community relationships? How has this changed over time?
- How are community partners included in the work of campus engagement? Are relationships organic and mutual? Do community partners feel included in campus decision making?
- What about impact? Does campus involvement in community work make a difference? What works, and what does not? Is service affecting community change? What could higher education be doing better?

Administrators. The research makes clear a need for an active commitment from administrators to encourage engagement, in addition to the need for support structures to affirm the commitment. There is concern that rhetoric regarding service and engagement does not match campus realities, but there has not been much research on the topic. Following are some questions to help shape a research agenda about administrators and their involvement with engagement:

- How do administrators reconcile the need for different types of scholarship to fulfill different needs of a campus? For research campuses, how does traditional research fit in when new forms of scholarship are added? For teaching campuses, how does involvement in service change things?
- In the light of concerns about lip-service to service, do administrators have mechanisms to let them know how they are doing with integration? Mechanisms to assess faculty level of commitment?
- Have administrators modified reward structures to recognize engagement? How have they made these modifications? Have these changes encouraged engagement?

- To what extent are department chairs supportive of engagement? What are their views on redefinitions of scholarship? How does this vary by institutional type?
- How do deans support their faculty in adopting a scholarship of engagement?

General. As researchers continue to look at general perspectives on service and how it is being integrated across the country, there are a variety of research questions that could help shape the future:

- How does institutional type factor in with integrating engagement? What lessons are there to be learned from different types of campus successes?
- What about community colleges? A lot of models about service-learning emerge from the community college sector but fewer about engagement. How can these models be integrated?
- What are the needs of campuses at different stages of the integration of engagement?
- What role do disciplinary associations play in awareness and integration of service? Does talking about it at national meetings make a difference?
- What role do professional organizations like the American Association for Higher Education and Campus Compact play in advancing the cause of engagement?
- How has conversation about engagement evolved? Are campuses critical about their own views of service, engagement, outreach, and the nuances of these definitions?
- What mechanisms are in place to assess matches in rhetoric and reality?
- To what extent is the Boyer model being used throughout the country? Are there other models in place as well?

Creating an engaged campus, where faculty internal and external service roles are defined and a broadened definition of scholarship is acknowledged, requires working internally to consider the mission and scope of a campus and its faculty and externally to address issues of the common good. Realizing goals for engagement calls for rethinking the position of higher education in relation to its multiple constituencies, answering the difficult questions about how to engage communities, and taking the risks necessary to make it happen. The engaged campus serves the common good by using its resources and expertise to answer challenges and needs both internal and external. Engagement is a difficult but noble goal. The engaged campus connects the campus to its past, unifies and focuses its present, and presents new opportunities for the future.

The engaged campus serves the common good by using its resources and expertise to answer challenges and needs both internal and external.

References

Aguirre, A. (2000). *Women and minority faculty in the academic workplace.* ASHE-ERIC Higher Education Report, Vol. 27, No. 6. San Francisco: Jossey-Bass.

Aldersley, S. F. (1995). "Upward drift" is alive and well: Research/doctoral model still attractive to institutions. *Change, 27*(5), 50–56.

Alger, J. R. (2000, Nov. 23). How to recruit and promote minority faculty: Start by playing fair. *Black Issues in Higher Education.*

Altbach, P. G. (1995). Problems and possibilities: The US academic profession. *Studies in Higher Education, 20,* 27–44.

Altbach, P. G. (1999). Patterns in higher education development. In P. G. Altbach, R. O. Berdahl, and P. J. Gumport (Eds.), *American higher education in the twenty-first century* (pp. 15–37). Baltimore: Johns Hopkins University Press.

American Council on Education. (1999). *To touch the future, transforming the way teachers are taught: An action agenda for college and university presidents.* Washington, DC: American Council on Education Fulfillment Service.

Antonio, A. L., Astin, H. S., and Cress, C. M. (2000). Community service in higher education: A look at the nation's faculty. *Review of Higher Education, 23*(4), 373–398.

Applegate, J. L., and Morreale, S. P. (2001). Creating engaged disciplines. *AAHE Bulletin,* pp. 7–9, 16.

Arches, J., and others. (1997). New voices in university-community transformation. *Change, 29*(1), 36–41.

Aronowitz, S. (2001). *The knowledge factory.* Boston: Beacon Press.

Astin, A. W. (1994, Jan.). *Higher education and the future of democracy.* Symposium conducted at the first annual Allan M. Carter Symposium, University of California–Los Angeles.

Astin, A. W., and Sax, L. J. (1998). How undergraduates are affected by service participation. *Journal of College Student Development, 39*(3), 251–63.

Austin, A. E. (2002). Preparing the next generation of faculty: Graduate school as socialization to the academic career. *Journal of Higher Education, 73*(1), 94–122.

Austin, A. E., and Gamson, Z. F. (1983). *Academic workplace: New demands, heightened tensions* ASHE-ERIC Higher Education Research Report No. 10. Washington, DC: George Washington University.

Ayers, G. E., and Ray, D. B. (Eds.). (1996). *Service learning: Listening to different voices.* Fairfax, VA: College Fund/UNCF.

Baez, B. (2000). Race-related service and faculty of color: Conceptualizing critical agency in academe. *Higher Education, 39,* 363–391.

Baldwin, R. G., and Blackburn, R. T. (1981). The academic career as a developmental process. *Journal of Higher Education, 52,* pp. 598–614.

Bell, S., and Jones, G. A. (1992). Paid consulting in Ontario Colleges of applied arts and technology. *Canadian Journal of Higher Education, 22*(3), 1–13.

Bensimon, E. M., Neumann, A., and Birnbaum, R. (1989). *Making sense of administrative leadership: The "L" word in higher education* ASHE-ERIC Higher Education Report, No. 1. Washington, DC: George Washington University.

Bensimon, E. M., Ward, K., and Sanders, K. (2000). *The department chair's role in developing new faculty into teachers and scholars.* Bolton, MA: Anker.

Benson, L., and Harkavy, I. (2000). Integrating the American system of higher, secondary, and primary education to develop civic responsibility. In T. Erlich, (Ed.), *Civic responsibility and higher education* (pp. 174–196). Phoenix, AZ: Oryx Press.

Berberet, J. (1999). The professoriate and institutional citizenship toward a scholarship of service. *Liberal Education, 85*(4), 33–39.

Berberet, J. (2002). The new academic compact. In L. A. McMillin and J. Berberet (Eds.), *The new academic compact: Revisioning the relationship between faculty and their institutions* (pp. 3–28). Bolton, MA: Anker.

Berdahl, R. O., Altbach, P. G., and Gumport, P. J. (1999b). The contexts of American higher education. In P. G. Altbach, R. O. Berdahl, and P. J. Gumport (Eds.), *American higher education in the twenty-first century* (pp. 1–11). Baltimore: Johns Hopkins University Press.

Boice, R. (1992). Quick starters. In M. Theall (Ed.), *Effective practices for improving teaching* (pp. 111–121). San Francisco: Jossey-Bass.

Boice, R. (1995). *The new faculty member.* San Francisco: Jossey-Bass.

Boice, R. (2000). *Advice for new faculty members: Nihil nimus.* Needham Heights, MA: Allyn & Bacon.

Boss, J. A. (1994). The effect of community service on the moral development of college ethics students. *Journal of Moral Education, 23*(2), 183–198.

Boyer, C. M., and Lewis, D. R. (1985). *And on the seventh day: Faculty consulting and supplemental income.* Washington, DC: National Institution of Education. (ED 262 743)

Boyer, E. L. (1990). *Scholarship reconsidered: Priorities of the professoriate.* Princeton, NJ: Carnegie Foundation for the Advancement of Teaching.

Boyer, E. L. (1994). Creating the new American college. *Chronicle of Higher Education, 40*(27), A48.

Boyer, E. L. (1996). The scholarship of engagement. *Journal of Public Service and Outreach, 1*(1), 11–20.

Boyte, H. C. (1999). Off the playground of civil society. *Good Society, 9*(2), 1–7.

Boyte, H. C., and Farr, J. (2000). The work of citizenship and the problem of service-learning. *Campus Compact Reader, 1*(1), 4.

Boyte, H. C., and Hollander, E. (1999). *Wingspread declaration on renewing the civic mission of the American research university.* Paper presented at the Wingspread Conference, Racine, WI. (ED 435 370)

Braskamp, L. A., and Wergin, J. F. (1998). Forming a new social partnership. In W. G. Tierney (Ed.), *The responsive university: Restructuring for high performance* (pp. 62–91). Baltimore: Johns Hopkins University Press.

Brawer, F. B. (1998). Academic entrepreneurship in higher education. *CELCEE Digest, 98*(3), 3–4.

Braxton, J. M., Luckey, W., and Helland, P. (2002). *Institutionalizing a broader view of scholarship into colleges and universities through Boyer's four domains.* ASHE-ERIC Higher Education Report, Vol. 29, No. 2. San Francisco: Jossey-Bass.

Bringle, R. G., Games, R., and Malloy, E. A. (Eds.). (1999). *Colleges and universities as citizens.* Needham Heights, MA: Allyn & Bacon.

Bringle, R. G., and Hatcher, J. A. (2000). Institutionalization of service learning in higher education. *Journal of Higher Education, 71*(3), 273–290.

Bringle, R. G., and Hatcher, J. A. (2002). Campus-community partnerships: The terms of engagement. *Journal of Social Issues, 58*(3), 503–516.

Bringle, R. G., Hatcher, J. A., Hamilton, S., and Young, P. (2001). Planning and assessing to improve campus-community engagement. *Metropolitan Universities: An International Forum, 12*(3), 89–99.

Brown, N. (1994). Community compacts: Models for metropolitan universities. *Metropolitan Universities: An International Forum, 4,* pp. 25–31.

Brubacher, J. S., and Rudy, W. (1997). *Higher education in transition: A history of American colleges and universities.* New Brunswick, NJ: Transaction.

Burack, C. (2000). Project colleague. *Academe, 86*(4), 43–45.

Burgan, M. (1998). Academic citizenship: A fading vision. *Liberal Education, 84*(4), 16–21.

Butler, J. E. (2000, July–Aug.). Democracy, diversity, and civic engagement. *Academe,* 52–55.

Byron, W. J. (2000). A religious-based college and university perspective. In T. Ehrlich (Ed.), *Civic responsibility and higher education* (pp. 279–294). Phoenix, AZ: Oryx Press.

Calderon, J. (1999, Sept.). Making a difference: Service-learning as an activism catalyst and community builder. *AAHE Bulletin, 52*(1), 7–9.

Cambridge, B. L. (1999). Effective assessment: A signal of quality citizenship. In R. G. Bringle, R. Games, and E. A. Malloy (Eds.), *Colleges and universities as citizens* (pp. 173–192). Needham Heights, MA: Allyn & Bacon.

Campbell, J. R. (1998). *Reclaiming a lost heritage: Land grant and other higher education initiatives for the twenty-first century.* Lansing, MI: Michigan State.

Caplow, T., and McGee, R. (2001 [originally published 1958, Basic]). *The academic market place.* New Brunswick, NJ: Transaction Publishers.

Carlisle, B. A., and Miller, M. T. (1998). *Current trends and issues in the practice of faculty involvement in governance.* Tuscaloosa, AL: National Data Base on Faculty Involvement in Governance. (ED 423 758)

Carnevale, A. P., and Desrochers, D. M. (2001). *Help wanted . . . credentials required.* Washington, DC: Educational Testing Service.

Carpenter, B., and Jacobs, J. (1994). Service learning: A new approach in higher education. *Education, 115*(1), 97–99.

Chaffee, E. E. (1997). Listening to the people you serve. In *Assessing Impact: Evidence and action. Presentations from the AAHE Conference on Assessment and Quality (Miami Beach, FL, June 11–15, 1997).* Washington, DC: American Association for Higher Education.

Chaffee, E. E. (1998). Listening to the people we serve. In W. G. Tierney (Ed.), *The responsive university: Restructuring for high performance* (pp. 13–37). Baltimore: Johns Hopkins University Press.

Checkoway, B. (1997). Reinventing the research university for public service. *Journal of Planning Literature, 11*(3), 307–320.

Checkoway, B. (2000). Public service: Our new mission. *Academe, 86*(4), 24–28.

Checkoway, B. (2001). Renewing the civic mission of the American research university. *Journal of Higher Education, 72*(2), 125–147.

Checkoway, B. (2002). *Creating the engaged campus.* Presentation at the annual meeting of the American Association for Higher Education, Faculty Roles and Rewards Conference, Phoenix, AZ.

Church, R. L. (2001, Nov.). *Counting public service: Can we make meaningful comparisons within and among institutions?* Paper presented at the ASHE Symposium on "Broadening the Carnegie Classification's Attention to Mission: Incorporating Public Service," Richmond, VA.

Church, R. L., and Sedlak, M. W. (1976). *Education in the United States: An interpretive history.* New York: Free Press.

Clark, B. R. (1983). Faculty: Differentiation and dispersion. In A. Levine (Ed.), *Higher learning in America.* Baltimore: Johns Hopkins University Press.

Clark, B. R. (1987). *The academic life: Small worlds, different worlds.* Princeton, NJ: Carnegie Foundation for the Advancement of Teaching.

Cohen, A. (1998). *The shaping of American higher education: Emergence and growth of the contemporary system.* San Francisco: Jossey-Bass.

Couto, R. A. (2001). The promise of a scholarship of engagement. *Academic Workplace, 12*(2), 4–7.

Cremin, L. A. (1970). *American education: The colonial experience.* New York: HarperCollins.

Crosson, P. (1983). *Public service in higher education: Practices and priorities* ASHE-ERIC Higher Education Research Report. Washington, DC: George Washington University. (ED 284 515)

Crosson, P. (1985). *Public service at public colleges.* Washington, DC: American Association of State Colleges and Universities.

Crosson, P. H. (1988, Nov.). *The study of public service in higher education.* Paper presented at the annual meeting of the Association for the Study of Higher Education, St. Louis, MO.

Cuban, L. (1999). *How scholars trumped teachers: Change without reform in university curriculum, teaching, and research, 1890–1990.* New York: Teachers College Press.

Curti, M., and Carstensen, V. (1949). *The University of Wisconsin.* Madison: University of Wisconsin.

Cushman, E. (1999). The public intellectual, service learning, and activist research. *College English, 61*(3), 328–336.

Diamond, R. M. (1999). *Aligning faculty rewards with institutional mission: Statements, policies and guidelines.* Bolton, MA: Anker.

Diamond, R. M., and Adam, B. E. (Eds.). (1995). *The disciplines speak: Rewarding the scholarly, professional, and creative work of faculty.* Washington, DC: American Association for Higher Education.

Dietrich, D. (1993, Mar.–Apr.). *Fringe benefits of writing consulting.* Paper presented at the Annual Meeting of the Conference on College Composition and Communication, San Diego, CA.

Dinham, S. M. (1987). *Between academe and professional practice: Initial reflections on analyzing the role of professional practice in higher education.* Paper presented at the 1987 Western Regional Meeting of the Association of Collegiate Schools of Architecture, Tucson, AZ. (ED 289 398)

Driscoll, A., and Lynton, E. A. (1999). *Making outreach visible: A guide to documenting professional service and outreach.* Washington, DC: American Association for Higher Education.

Driscoll, A., Sandmann, L., Foster-Fishman, P., and Bringle, R. (2000, Feb.). *Documenting the scholarship of engagement and practice: Advancing rewards for professional service and outreach.* Paper presented at the Eighth AAHE Conference on Faculty Roles and Rewards, New Orleans, LA.

Eason, A. (1996). *Job satisfaction for African American teachers in historically Black colleges and universities as compared with African American teachers in predominantly white colleges and universities.* Unpublished doctoral dissertation, Tennessee State University, Nashville.

Eby, J. W. (1996). Linking service and scholarship. In R. Sigmon (Ed.), *Journey to service learning* (pp. 87–98). Washington, DC: Council of Independent Colleges.

Eckel, P. D. (2000a). The role of shared governance in institutional hard decisions: Enabler or antagonist? *Review of Higher Education, 24*(1), 15–39.

Eckel, P. D. (2000b). Department chairs as institutional change leaders: Reframing "good chair leadership." *Academic Workplace, 11,* 4–7.

Edgerton, R. (1995a, Sept.). Bowling alone: How an erosion of social capital endangers American democracy. *AAHE Bulletin, 48*(1), 3–6.

Edgerton, R. (1995b, Sept.). Crossing boundaries: Pathways to productive learning and community renewal. *AAHE Bulletin, 48*(1), 7–10.

Edgerton, R., Hutchings, P., and Quinlan, K. (1991). *The teaching portfolio: Capturing the scholarship in teaching.* Washington, DC: American Association for Higher Education.

Ehrlich, T. (1995). Taking service seriously. *AAHE Bulletin, 47*(7), 8–10.

Ehrlich, T. (1999, June). Civic education: Lessons learned. *PS, Political Science and Politics, 32*(2), 245–249.

Ehrlich, T. (2000). *Civic responsibility and higher education.* Phoenix, AZ: Oryx Press.

Elman, S. E., and Smock, S. M. (1985). *Professional service and faculty rewards: Toward an integrated structure.* Washington, DC: National Association of State Universities and Land-Grant Colleges.

Elsner, P. A. (2000). A community college perspective. In T. Ehrlich (Ed.), *Civic responsibility and higher education* (pp. 211–226). Phoenix, AZ: Oryx Press.

Engstrom, C. M., and Tinto, V. (1997). Working together for service-learning. *About Campus, 2*(3), 10–15.

Ewell, P. T. (1991, Nov.–Dec.). Assessment and public accountability: Back to the future. *Change,* 12–17.

Ewell, P. T. (1994). Restoring our links with society: The neglected art of collective responsibility. *Metropolitan Universities: An International Forum, 5*(1), 79–87.

Eyler, J., and Giles, D. E., Jr. (1999). *Where's the service in service learning?* San Francisco: Jossey-Bass.

Fairweather, J. S. (1996). *Faculty work and public trust: Restoring the value of teaching and public service in American academic life.* Needham Heights, MA: Allyn & Bacon.

Fairweather, J. S. (2002). The mythologies of faculty productivity: Implications for institutional policy and decision-making. *Journal of Higher Education 73*(1), 26–48.

Farmer, J. A., and Schomberg, S. F. (1993). *A faculty guide for relating public service to the promotion and tenure review process.* Champaign-Urbana: University of Illinois.

Fear, F. A., and Sandmann, L. R. (1995). Unpacking the service category: Reconceptualizing university outreach for the 21st century. *Continuing Higher Education Review, 59*(3), 110–122.

Fear, F. A., and Sandmann, L. R. (1998). A legacy rediscovered: Public service at private colleges. *Journal of Public Service and Outreach, 3*(2), 48–53.

Fine, M., Weis, L., Weseen, S., and Wong, L. (2000). For whom? Qualitative research, representations and social responsibilities. In N. K. Denzin and Y. S. Lincoln (Eds.), *Handbook of qualitative research* (2nd ed., pp. 107–131). Thousand Oaks, CA: Sage.

Finkelstein, M. J. (1984). *The American academic profession: A synthesis of social scientific inquiry since World War II.* Columbus: Ohio State University Press.

Finkelstein, M. J., Seal, R. K., and Schuster, J. H. (1998). *The new academic generation: A profession in transformation.* Baltimore: Johns Hopkins University Press.

Finnegan, D. E. (1993). Segmentation in the academic labor market: Hiring cohorts in comprehensive universities. *Journal of Higher Education, 64,* pp. 621–656.

Finsen, L. (2002). Faculty as institutional citizens: Reconvening service and governance work. In L. A. McMillin and J. Berberet (Eds.), *The new academic compact: Revisioning the relationship between faculty and their institutions* (pp. 61–86). Bolton, MA: Anker.

Friedman, N. S. (1993). Getting the best of both worlds. In L. J. Zachary and S. Vernon (Eds.), *The Adult Educator as Consultant.* New Directions for Adult and Continuing Education, no. 58. San Francisco: Jossey-Bass.

Furco, A. (2002). Self assessment rubric for the institutionalization of service-learning in higher education. Berkeley, CA: Service-learning Research and Development Center.

Gamson, Z. F. (1997). Higher education and rebuilding civic life. *Change, 29*(1), 10–13.

Gamson, Z. F. (2000). Afterword: Defining the civic agenda for higher education. In T. Ehrlich (Ed.), *Civic responsibility and higher education* (pp. 367–372). Phoenix, AZ: Oryx Press.

Gamson, Z., Hollander, E., and Kiang, P. (1998). The university in engagement with society. *Liberal Education, 84*(2), 20–25.

Garcia, M. (Ed.). (2000). *Succeeding in an academic career: A guide for faculty of color.* Westport, CT: Greenwood Press.

Geiger, R. L. (1999). The ten generations of American higher education. In P. T. Altbach, R. O. Berdahl, and P. T. Gumport (Eds.), *American higher education in the 21st century: Social, political, and economic challenges* (pp. 38–69). Baltimore, MD: Johns Hopkins University Press.

Gelmon, S., and Agre-Kippenhan, S. (2002). Promotion, tenure, and the engaged scholar. *AAHE Bulletin, 54*(5), 7–11.

Glassick, C. E., Huber, M. T., and Maeroff, G. I. (1997). *Scholarship assessed: Evaluation of the professoriate.* San Francisco: Jossey-Bass.

Gray, M. J. (2000, May–June). Making the commitment to community service: What it takes. *About Campus, 5*(2), 19–24.

Gray, M., Ondaatje, E., Fricker, R., and Geschwind, S. (2000). Assessing service-learning. *Change, 32*(2), 30–40.

Grayson, D. A. (2001, Apr. 12). *Sisters and allies: Personal and professional journeys of women in educational research.* Paper presented at the American Educational Research Association Annual Meeting, Seattle, WA.

Gronski, R. (2000). University and community collaboration. *American Behavioral Scientist, 43*(5), 781–793.

Harkavy, I. (1993). Community service and the transformation of the American university. In S. Sagawa and S. Halperin (Eds.), *Visions of service: The future of the National and Community Service Act.* Washington, DC: National Women's Law Center and American Youth Policy Forum.

Harkavy, I. (1999, Fall-Winter). School-community-university partnerships: Effectively integrating community building and education reform. *Universities and Community Schools, 6*(1–2), 7–24.

Harkavy, I., and Puckett, J. L. (1994, Sept.). Lessons from Hull House for the contemporary urban university. *Social Service Review,* pp. 303–317.

Harris, F. C. (1998). Community service in academia. *Journal of General Education, 47*(4), 282–303.

Hesser, G. (1995, Fall). Faculty assessment of student learning: Outcomes attributed to service-learning and evidence of changes in faculty attitudes about experiential education. *Michigan Journal of Community Service Learning, 2,* 22–42.

Faculty Service Roles and the Scholarship of Engagement

Hill, D., and Pope, D. C. (1995, Apr.). *Establishing a beachhead: Service learning at Stanford. Are school-university-community partnerships worth the struggle? Service learning: A case study.* Paper presented at the annual meeting of the American Educational Research Association, San Francisco.

Hinck, S. S., and Brandell, M. E. (2000). The relationship between institutional support and campus acceptance of academic service learning. *American Behavioral Scientist, 43*(5), 868–882.

Hirose-Wong, S. M. (1999). *Gateways to democracy: Six urban community college systems* (Report No. EDO-JC-99–11). Washington, DC: Office of Educational Research and Improvement. (ED 438 873)

Hirsch, W. Z., and Weber, L. E. (1999). *Challenges facing higher education at the millennium.* Phoenix: American Council on Education and Oryx Press.

Hirsh, D., and Lynton, E. (1995). *Bridging two worlds: Professional service and service learning.* Boston: New England Resource Center for Higher Education, University of Massachusetts at Boston, Graduate College of Education.

Hoeveler, J. D. (1997). The university and the social gospel: The intellectual origins of the "Wisconsin idea." In L. F. Goodchild and H. S. Wechsler (Eds.), *The history of higher education* (4th ed., pp. 234–246). Needham Heights, MA: Allyn & Bacon.

Holland, B. A. (1997). Analyzing institutional commitment to service. *Michigan Journal of Community Service Learning, 4,* 30–41.

Holland, B. A. (1999). Factors and strategies that influence faculty involvement in public service. *Journal of Public Service and Outreach, 4*(1), 37–43.

Holland, B. A. (2001, Nov.). *Measuring the role of civic engagement in campus missions: Key concepts and challenges.* Paper presented at the ASHE Symposium "Broadening the Carnegie Classification's Attention to Mission: Incorporating Public Service," Richmond, VA.

Holland, B. A., and Gelmon, S. B. (1998). The state of the "engaged campus." *AAHE Bulletin, 51*(2), 3–6.

Hollander, E. L. (1998). *Picturing the engaged campus.* Providence, RI: Brown University, Campus Compact.

Hollander, E. L., and Saltmarsh, J. (2000). The engaged university. *Academe, 86*(4), 29–32.

Howsam, R. B. (1985). *Academic consulting in colleges and universities: Enclaves of intellectual and moral integrity.* Austin, TX: Texas College and University System. (ED 261 571)

Huber, M. T. (2001, July–Aug.). Balancing acts: Designing careers around the scholarship of teaching. *Change,* pp. 21–29.

Hy, R. J., Venhaus, M., and Sims, R. G. (1995, Sept.–Oct.). Academics in service to the legislature: Legislative utilization of college and university faculty and staff. *Public Administration Review, 55*(5), 468–474.

Jacoby, B. (1996). *Service learning in higher education: Concepts and practices.* San Francisco: Jossey-Bass.

Jay, G. (2000). The community in the classroom. *Academe, 86*(4), 33–37.

Jencks, C., and Riesman, D. (1977). *The academic revolution.* Chicago: University of Chicago Press.

Jones, D., Ewell, P., and McGuinness, A. (1998, Dec.). *The challenges and opportunities facing higher education.* San Jose, CA: National Center for Public Policy and Higher Education. (ED 426 643)

Kahne, J., and Westheimer, J. (1996). In the service of what? The politics of service learning. *Phi Delta Kappan, 77*(9), 593–599.

Keener, M. S. (1999). Strengthening institutional engagement: Addressing faculty issues to facilitate change. *Journal of Public Service and Outreach, 4*(1), 29–36.

Kellogg Commission on the Future of State and Land-Grant Universities. (1999a). *Engaged institutions: A commitment to service: Profiles and data.* Washington, DC: National Association of State Universities and Land Grant Colleges. (ED 430 499)

Kellogg Commission on the Future of State and Land-Grant Universities. (1999b). *Returning to our roots: The engaged institution.* Washington, DC: National Association of State Universities and Land Grant Colleges.

Kellogg Commission on the Future of State and Land-Grant Universities. (2000). *Renewing the covenant: Learning, discovery, and engagement in a new age and different world.* Washington, DC: National Association of State Universities and Land-Grant Colleges.

Kemmis, S., and McTaggart, R. (2000). Participatory action research. In N. K. Denzin and Y. S. Lincoln (Eds.), *Handbook of qualitative research* (2nd ed., pp. 567–605). Thousand Oaks, CA: Sage.

Kennedy, D. (1997). *Academic duty.* Cambridge, MA: Harvard University Press.

Kenworthy, A. L. (1996). Linking business education, campus culture and community: The Bentley service learning project. *Journal of Business Ethics, 15,* 121–131.

Kerr, C. (1963). *The uses of the university.* Cambridge, MA: Harvard.

Kezar, A. (2002). Assessing community service learning: Are we identifying the right outcomes? *About Campus, 7*(2), 14–20.

Kezar, A., and Rhoads, R. A. (2001). The dynamic tensions of service learning in higher education: A philosophical perspective. *Journal of Higher Education, 72*(2), 148–171.

Kolb, D. A. (1984). *Experiential education: Experience as the source of learning and development.* Englewood Cliffs, NJ: Prentice Hall.

Kolodny, A. (1998). *Failing the future: A dean looks at higher education in the twenty-first century.* Durham, NC: Duke University Press.

Lagemann, E. C. (1991). Purpose and public service: Thinking about research universities in the 1900s. *Teachers College Record, 92*(4), 523–528.

Lawson, H. (1990). Constraints on the professional service of education faculty. *Journal of Teacher Education, 41*(4), 57–71.

Lawson, J. C. (1996). Moonlighting becomes them: College faculty become entrepreneurs, high-priced consultants off-campus. *Black Issues in Higher Education, 13*(6), 24–25.

Leatherman, C. (1998, January 30). "Shared governance" under siege: Is it time to revive or get rid of it? *Chronicle of Higher Education,* p. A8.

Lee, L. (1997, Feb.). *Civic literacy, service learning, and community renewal* (Report No. EDO-JC-97-04). Washington, DC: Office of Educational Research and Improvement. (ED 405 913)

Leslie, D. W. (2002). Resolving the dispute: Teaching is academe's core value. *Journal of Higher Education, 73*(1), 49–73.

Light, D. (1972). The impact of the academic revolution on faculty careers. *ERIC-AAHE Research Report, No. 10.* Washington, DC: American Association for Higher Education.

Lords, E. (2000, 22 Sept.). A revolution in academic advising at a Texas community college. *Chronicle of Higher Education, 47*(4), A47-A48.

Lynton, E. A. (1995). *Making the case for professional service.* Washington, DC: American Association for Higher Education.

Lynton, E. A. (1998, Mar.). Reversing the telescope: Fitting individual tasks to common organizational ends. *AAHE Bulletin, 50*(7), 8–10.

Lynton, E. A., and Elman, S. E. (1987). *New priorities for the university: Meeting society's needs for applied knowledge and competent individuals.* San Francisco: Jossey-Bass.

Magrath, C. P. (1999). Engagement and the twenty-first century university. *Journal of Public Service and Outreach, 4*(1), 3–7.

Maloney, W. A. (2000). The community as a classroom. *Academe, 86*(4), 38–45.

Marullo, S., and Edwards, B. (2000). From charity to justice. *American Behavioral Scientist, 43*(5), 895–903.

Maurrasse, D. J. (2001). *Beyond the campus: How colleges and universities form partnerships with their communities.* New York: Routledge.

Mayfield, L., Hellwig, M., and Banks, B. (1999). The Chicago response to urban problems. *American Behavioral Scientist, 42*(5), 857–869.

McCormick, A. C. (2000, Jan.). Bringing the Carnegie classification into the 21st century. *AAHE Bulletin, 52*(5), 3–6, 16.

McDaniels, M. (2002). Experiential education. In J.J.F. Forest and K. Kinser (Eds.), *Higher education in the United States: An encyclopedia: Vol. 1: A–L* (pp. 207–209). Santa Barbara, CA: ABC-Clio.

McKeachie, W. J. (2002). *McKeachie's teaching tips: Strategies, research, and theory for college and university teachers* (11th ed.). Boston: Houghton Mifflin.

McMillin, L. A., and Berberet, W. G. (Eds.). (2002). *A new academic compact: Revisioning the relationship between faculty and their institutions.* Bolton, MA: Anker.

Melnick, R. (1999). University policy centers and institutes: The think tank as public service function. *Metropolitan Universities: An International Forum, 10*(1), 9–19.

Mettetal, G., and Bryant, D. (1996). Service learning research projects: Empowerment in students, faculty, and communities. *College Teaching, 44*(1), 24–28.

Miller, M. T. (1996). *The faculty forum: A case study in shared authority.* Unpublished manuscript, University of Alabama. (ED 401 774)

Miller, M. T., Vacik, S. M., and Benton, C. (1998). Community college faculty involvement in institutional governance. *Community College Journal of Research and Practice, 22,* 645–654.

Mirvis, P. H. (1996). Midlife as a consultant. In P. J. Frost and M. S. Taylor (Eds.), *Rhythms of academic life: Personal accounts of careers in academia* (pp. 361–369). Thousand Oaks, CA: Sage.

Modern Language Association (1996). *Making faculty work visible: Reinterpreting professional service, teaching, and research in the fields of language and literature.* New York: Modern Language Association.

Morphew, C. C. (2002). A rose by any other name: Which colleges became universities. *Review of Higher Education, 25*(2), 207–224.

National Commission on Excellence in Education (1983). *A nation at risk: The imperative for educational reform.* Washington, DC: Department of Education.

Oakes, J., and Rogers, J. (2001). The public responsibility of public schools of education. In W. G. Tierney (Ed.), *Faculty work in schools of education: Rethinking roles and rewards for the twentieth century* (pp. 9–27). Albany, NY: State University of New York Press.

O'Meara, K. A. (1997, Mar.). *Rewarding faculty professional service* (Working Paper No. 19). Boston: New England Resource Center for Higher Education, University of Massachusetts–Boston, Graduate College of Education.

O'Meara, K. A. (2002). Uncovering the values in faculty evaluation of service as scholarship. *Review of Higher Education, 26,* pp. 57–80.

Padilla, A. M. (May, 1994). Ethnic minority scholars, research, and mentoring: Current and future issues. *Educational Researcher, 23*(4), 24–27.

Parker, L. L., Greenbaum, D. A., and Pister, K. S. (2001, Jan.–Feb.). Rethinking the land-grant research university for the digital age. *Change, 33*(1), 12–17.

Parsons, M. H. (Oct. 1989). *Community colleges and civic literacy: The quest for values, ethics, and college renewal.* Paper presented at the annual Convention of the Virginia Community Colleges, Roanoke, VA. (ED 314 104)

Paulsen, M. B., and Feldman, K. A. (1995). Toward a reconceptualization of scholarship: A human action system with functional imperatives. *Journal of Higher Education, 66,* 615–640.

Perkins, L. M. (1997). The impact of the "cult of true womanhood" on the education of black women. In L. F. Goodchild and H. S. Wechsler (Eds.), *The history of higher education* (pp. 183–190). Needham Heights, MA: Allyn & Bacon.

Peterman, D. (2000). Service learning in community colleges. *Community College Journal of Research and Practice, 24*(4), 321–326.

Portland State University (1999). Mission Statement. [http://www.pdx.edu/psumission.phtml]. Access date: January 19, 2003.

Potts, D. B. (1977). College enthusiasm! as public response: 1800–1860. *Harvard Educational Review, 47*(1), 149–161.

Prince, G. S. Jr. (2000). A liberal arts college perspective. In T. Ehrlich (Ed.), *Civic responsibility and higher education* (pp. 249–262). Phoenix, AZ: Oryx Press.

Putnam, R. (1996). "Bowling alone": An interview with Robert Putnam about America's collapsing civic life. *AAHE Bulletin, 48,* 3–6.

Pyre, J.F.A. (1920). *Wisconsin.* New York: Oxford University Press.

Ramaley, J. A. (2000a). Embracing civic responsibility. *AAHE Bulletin, 52,* 9–13, 20.

Ramaley, J. A. (2000b). The perspective of a comprehensive university. In T. Ehrlich (Ed.), *Civic responsibility and higher education* (pp. 227–248). Phoenix, AZ: Oryx Press.

Ray, E. J. (1998). Outreach, engagement will keep academia relevant to twenty-first century societies. *Journal of Public Service and Outreach, 3,* 21–27.

Rhoads, R. A., and Howard, J.P.F. (Eds.) (1998). *Academic service learning: A pedagogy of action and reflection.* San Francisco: Jossey-Bass.

Rice, E. (1996a). *Making a place for the new American scholar.* Washington, DC: American Association for Higher Education.

Rice, E. (1996b). The academic profession in transition: Toward a new social fiction. In D. E. Finnegan, D. Webster, and Z. F. Gamson (Eds.), *Faculty and faculty issues in colleges and universities* (pp. 562–576). Boston: Pearson.

Richlin, L. (Ed.). (1993). *Preparing faculty for the new conceptions of scholarship.* New Directions for Teaching and Learning, No. 54. San Francisco: Jossey-Bass.

Riesman, D. (1980). *On higher education.* San Francisco: Jossey-Bass.

Roberts, A. O., Wergin, J. F., and Adam, B. E. (1993). Institutional approaches to the issues of reward and scholarship. In R. M. Diamond and B. E. Adam (Eds.), *Recognizing faculty work: Reward systems for the year 2000* (pp. 63–86). San Francisco: Jossey-Bass.

Robinson, G. (1999). *Community colleges broadening horizons through service learning* (Report No. AACC-PB-99-4). Washington, DC: Corporation for National Service. (ED 440 676)

Robinson, G. (2000). Stepping into our destiny: Service learning in community colleges. *Community College Journal, 70*(3), 8–12.

Rolls, J. A. (1998, Nov.). *Changing hats: Juggling the demands of academe and consulting/ training.* Paper presented at the Eighty-Fourth annual convention of the National Communication Association, New York.

Roschelle, A. R., Turpin, J., and Elias, R. (2000). Who learns from service learning? *American Behavioral Scientist, 43*(5), 839–848.

Rosentreter, F. M. (1957). *The boundaries of the campus.* Madison: University of Wisconsin Press.

Ross, R. G. (1997). *Faculty development programs: The communication professor as internal consultant.* Paper presented at the annual meeting of the National Communication Association, Chicago. (ED 420 888)

Rowley, L. L. (2001, Nov.). *Surveying the terrain: An exploratory analysis of the concept of public service in American higher education.* Paper presented at the ASHE Symposium on "Broadening the Carnegie Classification's Attention to Mission: Incorporating Public Service," Richmond, VA.

Saltmarsh, J. A. (2000, 02 May). Tomorrow's academy: The new university with a soul. Tomorrow's Professor listserv. Stanford University Learning Laboratory.

Saltmarsh, J. A., and Hollander, E. L. (1999). Off the playground of higher education. *Good Society, 9*(2), 28–31.

Sandmann, L. R., Foster-Fishman, P. G., Floyd, J., Rauhe, W., and Rosaen, C. (2000). Managing critical tensions: How to strengthen the scholarship component of outreach. *Change, 32*(1), 45–52.

Sax, L. J., and Astin, A. W. (1997, Summer–Fall). The benefits of service: Evidence from undergraduates. *Educational Record, 78*(3, 4), 25–32.

Schoenfeld, C. (1975). The "Wisconsin idea" expanded, 1949–1974. In A. G. Bogue and R. Taylor (Eds.), *The University of Wisconsin* (pp. 252–266). Madison: University of Wisconsin Press.

Scott, G.D.R. (2000). A historically black college perspective. In T. Ehrlich (Ed.), *Civic responsibility and higher education* (pp. 263–278). Phoenix, AZ: Oryx Press.

Sellery, G. C. (1960). *Some ferments at Wisconsin, 1901–1947.* Madison: University of Wisconsin.

Shulman, L. (1999). Course anatomy: The dissection and analysis of knowledge through teaching. In P. Hutchings (Ed.), *The course portfolio* (pp. 5–12). Washington, DC: American Association for Higher Education.

Singleton, S. E., Burack, C. A., and Hirsch, D. J. (1997). Faculty service enclaves. *AAHE Bulletin, 49*(8), 3–7.

Spanier, G. (2001, Feb. 22). *The engaged university: Our partnership with society.* Speech to the International Conference on the University as Citizen, University of South Florida, Tampa. [http://www.psu.edu/ur/GSpanier/speeches/engaged.html] Access date: Jan. 28, 2003.

Stanton, T. K. (1990). *Integrating public service with academic study: The faculty role.* Providence, RI: Brown University.

Stanton, T. K., Giles, D. E., and Cruz, N. I. (1999). *Service-learning: A movement's pioneers reflect on its origins, practice and future.* San Francisco: Jossey-Bass.

Sullivan, W. M. (2000). Institutional identity and social responsibility in higher education. In T. Erlich (Ed.), *Civic responsibility and higher education* (pp. 174–196). Phoenix, AZ: Oryx Press.

Sutton, T. P., and Bergerson, P. J. (2001). *Faculty compensation systems: The impact of the quality of education.* ASHE-ERIC Higher Education Report, Vol. 28, No. 2. San Francisco: Jossey-Bass.

Sykes, C. J. (1988). *ProfScam: Professors and the demise of higher education.* New York: St. Martin's Press.

Taylor, H. L. (1997). No more ivory towers: Connecting the research university to the community. *Journal of Planning Literature, 11*(3), 327–333.

Thomas, N. L. (1998). *The institution as a citizen: How colleges and universities enhance their civic roles.* (Working Paper No. 22). Boston: New England Resource Center for Higher Education, Graduate College of Education, University of Massachusetts.

Tierney, W. G. (Ed.). (1998). *The responsive university: Restructuring for high performance.* Baltimore, MD: Johns Hopkins University Press.

Tierney, W. G., and Bensimon, E. M. (1996). *Promotion and tenure: Community and socialization in academe.* Albany: State University of New York Press.

Townsend, B. K., and Turner, C. S. (2001). Reshaping the academy to accommodate conflicts of commitment: Then what? Paper presented at "Shaping a national agenda for women in higher education" conference. Minneapolis, MN.

Turner, C. S., and Myers, S. L. (2000). *Faculty of color in academe: Bittersweet success.* Needham, MA: Allyn & Bacon.

Turner, C.S.V. (2002). Women of color in the academe: Living with multiple marginality. *Journal of Higher Education, 73*(1), 74–93.

Udell, G. G. (1990). Academe and the goose that lays its golden egg. *Business Horizons, 33*(2), 29.

Van Hise, C. (1904). Inaugural address. In *The jubilee of the University of Wisconsin.* Madison: Jubilee Committee.

Vernon, A., and Ward, K. (1999). Campus and community partnerships: Assessing impacts and strengthening connections. *Michigan Journal of Community Service Learning, 6,* 30–37.

Veysey, L. R. (1965). *The emergence of the American university.* Chicago: University of Chicago Press.

Von Glinow, M. A. (1996). Working as a consultant: Academic imprimatur or taboo? In P. J. Frost and M. S. Taylor (Eds.), *Rhythms of academic life: Personal accounts of careers in academia* (pp. 372–379). Thousand Oaks, CA: Sage.

Votruba, J. C. (1996, Jan.–Feb.). The university's social covenant. *Adult Learning, 7*(3), 28–29.

Wagner, J. (1987, Sept.–Oct.). Teaching and research as student responsibilities: Integrating community and academic work. *Change, 19*(5), 26–35.

Walshok, M. L. (1995). *Knowledge without boundaries.* San Francisco: Jossey-Bass.

Walshok, M. L. (1997). *Strategies for building the infrastructure which supports the engaged university.* San Diego: University of California-San Diego.

Walshok, M. L. (2000). A research university perspective. In T. Ehrlich (Ed.), *Civic responsibility and higher education* (pp. 295–305). Phoenix, AZ: Oryx Press.

Walvrood, B. E., and others. (2000). *Academic departments: How they work, how they change.* ASHE-ERIC Higher Education Report, Vol. 27, No. 8. San Francicso: Jossey-Bass.

Ward, K. (1996). Service learning: Reflections on institutional commitment. *Michigan Journal of Community Service Learning, 3,* 55–65.

Ward, K. (1998). Addressing culture: Service learning, organizations, and faculty work. In R. A. Rhoads and J.P.F. Howard (Eds.), *Service learning: Theory and practice* (pp. 73–80). San Francisco: Jossey-Bass.

Ward, K. (2002). Service. In J. Forest and K. Kinser (Eds.), *Higher education in the United States: An encyclopedia.* Santa Barbara, CA: ABC-Clio.

Ward, K., and Wolf-Wendel, L. (2000). Community-centered service learning: Moving from doing for to doing with. *American Behavioral Scientist, 43*(5), 767–780.

Weidman, J. C., Twale, D. J., and Stein, E. L. (2001). *The socialization of graduate and professional students in higher education.* ASHE-ERIC Report, Vol. 28, No. 3. San Francisco: Jossey-Bass.

Weissman, R. (1988, Nov.). *Scholars, Inc.: Harvard academics in service of industry and government.* Cambridge, MA: Harvard. (ED 316 172).

Westbrook, F. D., and others. (1993, July–Aug.). University campus consultation: Opportunities and limitations. *Journal of Counseling and Development, 71,* 684–688.

Wildman, P. (1998). From the monophonic university to polyphonic multiversities. *Futures, 30*(7), 625–633.

Williams, D. (2000, Jan.). *Scholarship of service and teaching: Documentation and integration.* Unpublished manuscript, Portland State University.

Williams, F. (1996, 18 Mar.). Helping a busted mining town back to its feet. *High Country News,* p. 1.

Wong, P. W., and Tierney, W. G. (2001). Reforming faculty work: Culture, structure and the dilemma of organization. *Teachers College Record, 103*(6), 1081–1101.

Wright, B. (1988). "For the children of the infidels"? American Indian education in the colonial colleges. *American Indian Culture and Research Journal, 12*(3), 1–14.

Zahorski, K. J., Cognard, R., and Gilliard, M. D. (Eds.). (1999). *Reconsidering faculty roles and rewards: Promising practices for institutional transformation and enhanced learning.* Washington, DC: Council of Independent Colleges.

Zemsky, R. (1994). Certainly we have to get off our high horses. *Education Week, 13*(29), 20–22.

Zlotkowski, E. (1997). Service learning and the process of academic renewal. *Journal of Public Service and Outreach, 2*(1), 80–87.

Zlotkowski, E. (2000). Civic engagement and the academic disciplines. In T. Ehrlich (Ed.), *Civic responsibility and higher education* (pp. 309–322). Phoenix, AZ: Oryx Press.

Zlotkowski, E. (2001, Jan.–Feb.). Mapping new terrain: Service-learning across the disciplines. *Change, 33*(1), 25–33.

Name Index

Carnevale, A. P., 85
Carpenter, B., 118
Carstense, V., 29, 31
Chaffee, E. E., 9, 44, 48
Checkoway, B., 14, 45, 89, 90, 112, 137
Church, R. L., 92, 93
Clark, B. R., 17, 32, 33, 39, 40, 43, 47, 53, 57, 60, 61, 63, 64, 86, 93, 94, 121
Cognard, R., 137
Cohen, A., 7, 8, 18, 19, 20, 23, 24, 32, 33, 34, 35, 36, 38, 39, 40, 42, 45, 53, 54, 85, 86
Commons, J., 30
Couto, R. A., 81
Cremin, L. A., 18, 19
Cress, C. M., 11, 48, 97, 120
Crosson, P., 2, 52, 85, 87
Cruz, N. I., 38, 46
Cuban, L., 23, 28, 40, 41, 42, 47, 48, 106
Curti, M., 29, 31
Cushman, E., 78, 79, 80, 130, 131

D

Desrochers, D. M., 85
Diamond, R. M., 63, 93, 101, 102, 103, 104, 107, 108, 110, 121, 135
Dietrich, D., 75
Dinham, S. M., 94
Driscoll, A., 81, 103, 116, 128, 129

E

Eason, A., 60
Eby, J. W., 88, 104
Eckel, P. D., 54, 95
Edgerton, R., 45, 111, 112, 118
Edwards, B., 19
Ehrlich, T., 14, 69, 118
Elias, R., 118
Eliot, C., 28
Elman, S. E., 5, 52, 70, 72, 74, 75, 106, 124
Elsner, P. A., 85
Ely, R., 30
Engstrom, C. M., 118

Ewell, P. T., 119
Eyler, J., 79, 117, 118

F

Fairweather, J. S., 11, 40, 48, 57, 62, 104
Farr, J., 45, 48, 118
Fear, F. A., 2, 5, 15, 52, 54, 70, 88, 89, 131
Feldman, K. A., 106
Fine, M., 82
Finkelstein, M. J., 3, 14, 19, 20, 22, 23, 24, 32, 34, 35, 38, 47, 49, 53, 64, 69, 105
Finnegan, D. E., 86, 90
Finsen, L., 55, 56, 120, 121, 122, 130
Foster-Fishman, P., 81, 129
Franklin, B., 19
Fricker, R., 79
Friedman, N. S., 76, 77, 96
Furco, A., 141

G

Games, R., 10, 12, 14
Gamson, Z. F., 52, 56, 61, 64, 84, 90, 104, 107, 119, 127
Garcia, M., 60, 66
Geertz, C., 115
Geiger, R. L., 18, 20, 21, 26, 29, 33, 35, 89
Gelmon, S., 81, 116, 129
Geschwind, S., 79
Giles, D. E., 38, 46, 79, 117, 118
Gilliard, M. D., 137
Gilman, D. C., 28
Glassick, C. E., 108, 110, 111, 116, 128, 140
Gray, M., 79, 117, 125
Greenbaum, D. A., 72
Gumport, P. J., 44

H

Hamilton, S., 116, 117, 129
Harkavy, I., 5, 6, 10, 11, 13, 31, 32, 34
Harris, F. C., 98
Hatcher, J. A., 116, 117, 121, 125, 129
Helland, P., 12, 104
Hellwig, M., 34, 73, 87
Hesser, G., 79, 117, 118, 121

Hill, D., 63
Hinck, S. S., 125
Hirose-Wong, S. M., 85
Hirsch, D., 3, 5, 9, 79, 99, 124
Hoeveler, J. D., 29, 30
Holland, B. A., 4, 92, 93, 116, 120, 121, 125, 128, 141
Hollander, E. L., 2, 4, 12, 14, 90, 119
Howard, J.P.F., 78
Howsam, R. B., 76, 77
Huber, M. T., 108, 110, 116, 122, 123, 124, 128, 135
Hutchings, P., 104, 111
Hy, R. J., 77

J

Jacobs, J., 118
Jacoby, B., 46, 48, 78
Jay, G., 79
Jefferson, T., 19, 25
Jencks, C., 105, 107
Jones, G. A., 76

K

Kahne, J., 19
Keener, M. S., 90
Kemmis, S., 81
Kennedy, D., 7, 56, 90
Kerr, C., 19, 25, 27, 28, 38, 40, 44
Kezar, A., 79, 95, 117, 118, 119
Kiang, P., 119
Kolb, D. A., 8, 9, 40
Kolodny, A., 6, 7, 8, 9, 14, 66

L

Lagemann, E. C., 90
Lawson, H., 63, 74, 95, 96
Leatherman, C., 56
Lee, L., 85
Leslie, D. W., 62, 63, 104
Lewis, D. R., 74, 75, 77, 127
Light, D., 23
Lords, E., 58
Luckey, W., 12, 104
Lynton, E., 2, 5, 15, 52, 69, 70, 72, 74,

75, 76, 79, 84, 103, 104, 106, 113, 115, 116, 124, 128, 129, 130, 136, 141

M

Madison, J., 25
Maeroff, G. I., 108, 110, 116, 128
Magrath, C. P., 13, 14, 15, 79, 91
Malloy, E. A., 10, 12, 14
Maloney, W. A., 79
Marullo, S., 19
Maurrasse, D. J., 13, 14, 19, 27, 129
Mayfield, L., 34, 73, 87
McCarthy, D. C., 30
McCormick, A. C., 92, 93
McDaniels, M., 40, 48
McGee, R., 39, 106
McKeachie, W. J., 9
McKenna, M., 78, 82
McMillin, L. A., 53
McTaggart, R., 81
Mead, G. H., 34
Melnick, R., 77
Mettetal, G., 78
Miller, M. T., 43, 54, 56, 62, 121
Mirvis, P. H., 75
Monroe, J., 25
Morphew, C. C., 41, 90
Morreale, S. P., 93
Myers, S. L., 60, 66, 97

N

Neumann, A., 62

O

Oakes, J., 19, 95, 96
O'Meara, K. A., 15, 52, 60, 69, 79, 95, 97, 99, 107, 111, 112, 120, 121, 134, 137
Ondaatje, E., 79

P

Padilla, A. M., 66, 97
Parker, L. L., 72
Parsons, M. H., 86

Weseen, S., 82
Westheimer, J., 19
Wildman, P., 94
Williams, D., 81
Williams, F., 72
Wolf-Wendel, L., 13, 91, 129
Wong, L., 82
Wong, P. W., 53, 120
Wright, B., 18

Y

Young, P., 116, 117, 129

Z

Zahorski, K. J., 137
Zemsky, R., 11
Zlotkowski, E., 10, 64, 79, 81, 93, 94, 95

Subject Index

ASHE-ERIC
Higher Education Reports

The mission of the Educational Resources Information Center (ERIC) system is to improve American education by increasing and facilitating the use of educational research and information on practice in the activities of learning, teaching, educational decision making, and research, wherever and whenever these activities take place.

Since 1983, the ASHE-ERIC Higher Education Report series has been published in cooperation with the Association for the Study of Higher Education (ASHE). Starting in 2000, the series has been published by Jossey-Bass in conjunction with the ERIC Clearinghouse on Higher Education.

Each monograph is the definitive analysis of a tough higher education problem, based on thorough research of pertinent literature and institutional experiences. Topics are identified by a national survey. Noted practitioners and scholars are then commissioned to write the reports, with experts providing critical reviews of each manuscript before publication.

Six monographs in the series are published each year and are available on individual and subscription bases. To order, use the order form at the back of this issue.

Qualified persons interested in writing a monograph for the series are invited to submit a proposal to the National Advisory Board. As the preeminent literature review and issue analysis series in higher education, the Higher Education Reports are guaranteed wide dissemination and provide national exposure for accepted candidates. Execution of a monograph requires at least a minimal familiarity with the ERIC database, including *Resources in Education* and the current *Index to Journals in Education*. The objective of these reports is to bridge conventional wisdom and practical research.

Advisory Board

Consulting Editors
and Review Panelists

Barbara Holland
National Service Learning
Clearinghouse
Cathy Burack
New England Resource Center for
Higher Education, University of
Massachusetts—Boston
KerryAnn O'Meara
University of Massachusetts
John Braxton
Peabody College

Jim Palmer
Illinois State University
Judith Glazer Raymo
Long Island University
Linda Johnsrud
University of Hawaii at Manoa
Emilia E. Martinez-Brawley
Arizona State University

Recent Titles

Back Issue/Subscription Order Form

Copy or detach and send to:

Jossey-Bass, A Wiley Company, 989 Market Street, San Francisco CA 94103-1741

Call or fax toll-free: Phone 888-378-2537 6:30AM – 3PM PST; Fax 888-481-2665

Back Issues: Please send me the following issues at $24 each
(Important: please include series abbreviation and issue number.
For example AEHE28:1)

_____

_____

_____

$ _____   Total for single issues

$ _____   SHIPPING CHARGES: SURFACE   Domestic Canadian

	First Item	$5.00	$6.00
	Each Add'l Item	$3.00	$1.50

For next-day and second-day delivery rates, call the number listed above.

Subscriptions   Please ❏ start ❏ renew my subscription to *ASHE-ERIC Higher Education Reports* for the year 2____at the following rate:

U.S.	❏ Individual $150	❏ Institutional $150
Canada	❏ Individual $150	❏ Institutional $230
All Others	❏ Individual $198	❏ Institutional $261
Online Subscription		❏ Institutional $150

**For more information about online subscriptions visit
www.interscience.wiley.com**

$ _____   Total single issues and subscriptions (Add appropriate sales tax for your state for single issue orders. No sales tax for U.S. subscriptions. Canadian residents, add GST for subscriptions and single issues.)

❏Payment enclosed (U.S. check or money order only)
❏VISA ❏ MC ❏ Amex ❏ Discover Card #_____ Exp. Date _____

Signature _____ Day Phone _____
❏ Bill Me (U.S. institutional orders only. Purchase order required.)

Purchase order # _____
      Federal Tax ID13559302   **GST 89102 8052**

Name _____

Address _____

_____

Phone _____ E-mail _____

For more information about Jossey-Bass, visit our Web site at www.josseybass.com

PROMOTION CODE ND03

ASHE-ERIC HIGHER EDUCATION REPORT IS NOW AVAILABLE ONLINE AT WILEY INTERSCIENCE

What is Wiley InterScience?

Wiley InterScience is the dynamic online content service from John Wiley & Sons delivering the full text of over 300 leading scientific, technical, medical, and professional journals, plus major reference works, the acclaimed Current Protocols laboratory manuals, and even the full text of select Wiley print books online.

What are some special features of Wiley InterScience?

Wiley Interscience Alerts is a service that delivers table of contents via e-mail for any journal available on Wiley InterScience as soon as a new issue is published online.

Early View is Wiley's exclusive service presenting individual articles online as soon as they are ready, even before the release of the compiled print issue. These articles are complete, peer-reviewed, and citable.

CrossRef is the innovative multi-publisher reference linking system enabling readers to move seamlessly from a reference in a journal article to the cited publication, typically located on a different server and published by a different publisher.

How can I access Wiley InterScience?

Visit http://www.interscience.wiley.com.

Guest Users can browse Wiley InterScience for unrestricted access to journal Tables of Contents and Article Abstracts, or use the powerful search engine. *Registered Users* are provided with a *Personal Home Page* to store and manage customized alerts, searches, and links to favorite journals and articles. Additionally, Registered Users can view free Online Sample Issues and preview selected material from major reference works. *Licensed Customers* are entitled to access full-text journal articles in PDF, with select journals also offering full-text HTML.

How do I become an Authorized User?

Authorized Users are individuals authorized by a paying Customer to have access to the journals in Wiley InterScience. For example, a University that subscribes to Wiley journals is considered to be the Customer. Faculty, staff and students authorized by the University to have access to those journals in Wiley InterScience are Authorized Users. Users should contact their Library for information on which Wiley journals they have access to in Wiley InterScience.

ASK YOUR INSTITUTION ABOUT WILEY INTERSCIENCE TODAY!

Kelly Ward is an assistant professor in higher education at Washington State University in Pullman. Her research interests are faculty development, service-learning, faculty roles and rewards, and work and family in higher education. She has worked as an administrator in the areas of faculty development and service-learning and has held positions at the University of Montana and Oklahoma State University. She received her Ph.D. in higher education from Penn State University.